Big Data: Measuring the Digital Economy

Jemison

Contents

1 Introduction   **1**

     1.1   Internet, Big Data and Economic Indicators . . . .

         1.1.1   Evolution in Internet use and the WWW . . . .

         1.1.2   Internet and Big Data . . . .

         1.1.3   Economic indicators . . . .

         1.1.4   Online-based Big Data to produce economic indicators .

     1.2   Motivation . . . .

     1.3   Hypotheses and objectives . . . .

     1.4   Structure of the book . . . .

2 Big Data sources and methods for social and economic analyses   **19**

     2.1   Introduction . . . .

     2.2   Related work . . . .

     2.3   Non-traditional sources of social and economic data . . . . . .

         2.3.1   The Internet as basic means for generating socio-economic data . . . .

         2.3.2   Urban and mobile sensors . . . .

     2.4   Non-traditional methods for processing social and economic data

         2.4.1   Methods for structuring data . . . .

         2.4.2   Methods for modelling data . . . .

         2.4.3   Methods for assessing models' performance and robustness

     2.5   The data lifecycle . . . .

CONTENTS

  2.6 A Big Data Architecture for nowcasting and forecasting social and economic changes

      2.6.1 Data analysis layer

      2.6.2 Governance layer

      2.6.3 Persistence layer

  2.7 Conclusions

3 Web data mining for monitoring business export orientation 62

  3.1 Introduction

  3.2 Theoretical background

      3.2.1 Web data mining for science and economic indicators

      3.2.2 Export-related indicators built from website features

      3.2.3 Structural variables related to export orientation

  3.3 Using web-based variables to infer firm export orientation

      3.3.1 The sample

      3.3.2 Data analysis

      3.3.3 The predictive models

  3.4 Automating the retrieval of web-based variables

      3.4.1 Architecture of the web data mining system for analyzing corporate websites

      3.4.2 Construction and validation of automatic web-based variables

      3.4.3 Predicting firm export orientation from automatic web-based variables

  3.5 Conclusions

4 Monitoring e-commerce adoption from online data 91

  4.1 Introduction

  4.2 Related work

  4.3 SAME: a system for detecting and monitoring e-commerce adoption

      4.3.1 The capture module

4.3.2   The analysis module . . . .

4.3.3   The production module . . . .

4.4 Experimental results . . . .

4.4.1   Data . . . .

4.4.2   Results . . . .

4.5 Conclusions . . . .

5 Do corporate websites' changes reflect firms' survival?   118

5.1 Introduction . . . .

5.2 Theoretical background . . . .

5.2.1   Firms' survival analysis . . . .

5.2.2   Capturing firms' economic activities through web data .

5.3 Data and methodology . . . .

5.3.1   Data . . . .

5.3.2   Multi-period logistic regression . . . .

5.3.3   Survival analysis . . . .

5.4 Results . . . .

5.4.1   Descriptive statistics and group comparisons . . . . .

5.4.2   Multi-period logistic regression models . . . .

5.4.3   Survival analysis . . . .

5.5 Conclusions . . . .

6 Conclusions   141

6.1 Main contributions . . . .

6.2 Implications . . . .

6.3 Limitations . . . .

6.4 Future work . . . .

Chapter 1

Introduction

1.1 Internet, Big Data and Economic Indicators

The Internet and the WWW have revolutionized the way of operating and interacting in the economy and the society. The increasing use of the Internet by part of individuals, firms and governments, along with the expanding access to digital devices have contributed to the explosion of social and economic data generation. At the same time, thanks to the continuous advances in computation and analytics, these massive quantities of fresh, granular and digitized data, commonly referred to as "Big Data", can be properly processed and analyzed. Being highly related to social and economic behaviors, their potential for producing fast, up-to-date indicators useful for decision-making is enormous. Although research efforts in this line are increasing, there is still a long way to go regarding the understanding of online data to infer offline phenomena, and this is a necessary step to put them into production for providing regular forecasts and nowcasts about economic topics of relevance.

1.1.1 Evolution in Internet use and the WWW

The first approach to the Internet as we currently know it was released during the 1980s, after many research and implementation efforts performed since year 1958 in which the United States created the *Defense Advanced Research*

Projects Agency (DARPA) that was in charge of creating a network to interconnect computers. Along with teams of the Massachusetts Institute of Technology (MIT), the National Physics Laboratory of the United Kingdom and the Rand Corporation, in 1969 the first nerwork of computers was created, called *ARPANET*. This network adopted the "Transmission Control Protocol/Internet Protocol" (TCP/IP) protocol around 1983, a protocol to transmit information through the Internet that is the same type of technology used nowadays. However, it was not until the public release of the WWW in 1991, created by Tim Berners-Lee at CERN, when the use of the Internet really started to grow. To regulate its standards and protocols worldwide, the World Wide Web Consortium (W3C) was created in 1995 (Leiner et al., 1997; World Wide Web Foundation, 2018).

In short, the WWW is an information space where documents and a wide variety of web resources are hosted, and can be accessed through the Internet by using web browsers and web-based applications; it can also be described as a way of viewing the online information available on the Internet (Berners-Lee et al., 1993; Berners-Lee and Fischetti, 2001). The WWW made the use of the Internet much easier and intuitive, therefore helping to spread it.

Indeed, the Internet worldwide penetration rate increased from 6.8% in year 2000 to 54.4% in 2017, reaching a total of 4.1 billion users. However, Internet penetration differs importantly among the different regions of the world. As expected, the highest penetration rate (95%) corresponds to North America, while the lowest (35.2%) corresponds to Africa. Regarding the rest of regions, nearly 50% of the population at Asia use the Internet, while this percentage increases to around 65%-70% for Middle East, Australia and Latin America. In the case of Europe, in which this study is focused, 85.2% of the population used the Internet, which can be considered relatively high (Internet Live Stats, 2018a; Miniwatts Marketing Group, 2018). It is important to highlight that although the levels of penetration of the Internet among the different world regions vary, in all cases they have followed an increasing tendency in the last years, pointing out that Internet use continues expanding throughout the world.

At the same time that the number of Internet users have been increasing, the number of existing websites have increased too. The number of active websites, which are more representative of the real expansion of the Internet than the number of hostnames, increased from 10 million in December 2000 to 172 million in December 2017, although in the last 4 years the quantity of active websites seems to have become stagnant (Netcraft, 2018).

These patterns have largely influenced the way of operating of firms, for which the Internet and the WWW have turned out into basic tools for communicating, performing marketing actions and selling their products or services through e-commerce, among others. Indeed, in year 2017 around 93% of firms (small, medium and big, that is, firms with at least 10 workers) in the European Union (EU) had an internet connection, while 77% also had a website (Eurostat, 2018). Given that websites constitute the first tool for firms to establish their official public image on the Internet, it can be seen that a really high percentage of firms have decided to go online, something which is crucial in the current Digital Era.

In the case of Spain, for which most of the research presented in this book is done, in the first semester of year 2017 a total of 98.70% of their small, medium and big firms had an internet connection, while 77.69% also had a website, being in line with the figures of the EU presented above. It is also remarkable that in 2016, which is the most recent year for which data are available, 49.57% used social networking sites, and about e-commerce, 20.41%sold their products or services online while 31.36% did some online purchases. However, for the micro-enterprises, those with less than 10 workers, all of these percentages are lower. For instance, 70.22% had an internet connection, while only 29.81% also had a website (INE, 2017).

This shows that there is a long way to go in the adoption and use of the Internet and particularly, the WWW, in the business sector. Remarkably, all of the figures mentioned in this section have been increasing in the last years, reflecting that the tendency to adopt and use Internet as well as advanced online tools, is positive.

1.1.2 Internet and Big Data

The widespread use of the Internet by millions of people and companies world-wide have turned it into an important data generator tool. The tons of digitized, fresh data that are generated on a daily basis, which can be referred to with the term "Big Data", constitute a record of the transactions and behaviors of individuals and firms. If properly tracked, accessed and analyzed, these data could help to improve our knowledge and predictions about social and economic aspects (Askitas and Zimmermann, 2015). Their potential for social and economic research is reviewed in detail in Chapter 2 of this book, although much more of it is expected to be revealed in the following years as the use of the Internet, the WWW and social networks continue to expand and data analysis techniques continue to develop.

The concept of Big Data appeared for the first time in year 1997 in a paper written by researchers from the Intel Corporation and the NASA (Cox and Ellsworth, 1997). This work emphasized the increasing sizes of data available and explained how to treat them for data visualization. Some years later, in 2001, the first scientific definition of the term was done by means of the "3Vs" model (Laney, 2001), which described Big Data not only by their size, but also by the fast speed on data generation and their wide range of types and characteristics. The 3Vs model, which have been widely used, includes the following variables:

- **Volume**: This makes reference to the size or magnitude of data, which in the case of Big Data, is generally large. Daily data generation has been recently estimated in 2.5 exabytes (IBM, 2016), where each exabyte is equivalent to 10^6 terabytes. This is an aggregated, impressive figure; however, a threshold to determine if the volume of a particular data set is "big enough" to be considered Big Data has not been established. The concept of Big Data entails a complexity and heterogeneity that makes it difficult to establish a threshold, given that its definition may vary depending on the type of data, the moment of time (Big Data of today will not be the same as in 5 or 10 years) or the most proper way to store them, as depending on their type bigger or smaller databases would be necessary (Gandomi and Haider, 2015).

- **Velocity**: This refers to the speed in data generation and transfer. In a context in which digital devices (such as computers, smartphones, payment terminals or industrial machinery with sensors) are commonly used in a wide range of social and business activities, data are generated at a high speed, in real time. For instance, currently more than 500 million tweets are daily published on Twitter, with an average of 6,000 tweets per second (Internet Live Stats, 2018b). Thus, there is an increasing need to be prepared for storing, processing and analyzing these data in real time to make the most of them. Treating them properly, we may obtain advanced, accurate forecasts about economic and social variables that would help in decision-making, evidence-based planning and creating real value for customers (Gandomi and Haider, 2015).

- **Variety**: This refers to the wide range of types and structures of data that exist, which are originated from a variety of sources. About the types or formats, data may be, for instance, plain text, documents, images, video or audio files, encoded in different ways (e.g., .pdf, .csv, .xlsx, .json or .jpg). Regarding the structures, data may come structured (tabular data prepared for relational databases), semi-structured (data with machine-readable tags that do not follow a strict standard) or unstructured (data without a specific scheme to allow machines to read them, e.g. a video). Additionally, the number of different sources from which data may be originated has multiplied in the last years, ranging from any kind of sensor (in industrial machinery, shops, tolls, mobiles, smart clothes, etc.) to online-based resources (such as websites, blogs or social networks).

This model was revised by its author in 2012, defining Big Data as follows: "Big data is high volume, high velocity, and/or high variety information assets that require new forms of processing to enable enhanced decision making, insight discovery and process optimization" (Beyer and Laney, 2012). This definition highlights the process of extracting valuable information from data and, in line with this, the model was extended to include two additional "V" dimensions (Marr, 2015; Bello-Orgaz et al., 2016):

- **Veracity**: This makes reference to the accuracy and correctness of Big Data, as they may be messy, include noise, errors and uncertainty. The reasons behind this include basically the errors (from machines or individuals) in retrieving, storing and/or processing data; and the inaccuracy or uncertainty in the data itself (think, for instance, of data from social media in which individuals express their personal opinions: they may lie, express something wrongly or make typing errors, among others). To deal with these issues and assure veracity in the information obtained, proper, robust analytics and a reliable data governance system that takes into account privacy concerns, are needed.

- **Value**: This makes reference to the useful, granular and fresh information that can be extracted from Big Data, which may help not only businesses, but also policy makers, to make earlier, more informed decisions. To do so, specific techniques to process and analyze data with the particularities described above are required. These are known as "Big Data Analytics".

These five characteristics make Big Data potentially useful, but also imply a number of challenges for transforming them into valuable information for decision making. Among these, the process of extracting knowledge from Big Data to infer social and economic real information is one of the most important. Social and economic Big Data only capture a part of the offline reality, given that not every individual uses the Internet or digital devices (for instance, card readers if they pay in cash instead of with credit card), and not every firm has online activity or tracks its production processes (although this is increasingly being done). Therefore, issues of representativeness, bias and inference appear (Cox et al., 2018), and should be taken into account when generalizing the results from a particular data set.

Another challenge comes from deciding the frequency of data retrieval and analysis. This depends on a variety of aspects, including: the pace at which data change or new data are generated; the predictable time horizon, which could make reference to the present (including very recent past or very near future, as nowcasting does) or to longer periods (forecasting); and also, the type of economic indicator which is being produced. The latter affects because according to its purpose and the type of decisions that can be taken based on its results, the optimal frequency to retrieve fresh data and to update the indicator could differ. Therefore, implementing systems that provide us with the flexibility to program different frequencies for different indicators, and that allow to quickly change these frequencies when needed, is basic. Selecting which data to store is also an important challenge, given that daily data generation is higher than our technical capacity to store them. Thus, for each particular real case it would be appealing to study which data are necessary to store and for which reasons, and which are expendable.

Besides these challenges, particularly in the case of Big Data originated in the Internet, in which this **book** is focused, some of the most important issues to be taken into account include: the format of data (generally unstructured); the variety of sources that generate data (websites, blogs, social networking sites, search engines...), as this makes data integration a big challenge; and the reliability and bias existing in online data, given that not every individual, firm or organization currently use the Internet, and that who use it, may post inaccurate, incomplete or false information, as documented by Beresewicz et al. (2018).

In spite of that, online data has a big positive side that makes them worth: the digital footprint left by users on the Internet contains an unprecedented power to discover social and economic behaviors, with which we can provide of nowcasts and forecasts helpful for decision making and cost savings. Big Data analysis, thus, is necessary. In this **book** we have applied some of these analysis techniques to transform web data into useful information about eco-nomic variables. These, as explained in the following section, include: firm export orientation, firm enrollment in e-commerce and business demography.

1.1.3 Economic indicators

Indicators are intermediaries that link statistical observations with any kind of phenomena (Horn, 1993). Thus, and more specifically, an economic indicator can be defined as a statistical measure about an economic activity that allows to analyze its recent and past performance and helps to provide forecasts about such activity for the future.

The history of economic indicators is considered to start during the late 1930s and the 1940s. After some years of work, in 1947 the National Bureau of Economic Research (NBER) published a book that included a compilation of indicators about the status of the economic cycle of the United States, classified into three categories depending on the time moment their value change with respect to the economic cycle: leading, coincident and lagging indicators (Burns and Mitchell, 1947). Leading indicators are those that help to anticipate future events; coincident indicators reflect magnitudes that happen at the same time as a condition in the economy; while lagging indicators help to confirm past events. This classification still prevails and, since it was proposed, a wide range of indicators to measure the variety of economic variables that exist have been developed, particularly from a macroeconomics point of view, and ranging from a global to a regional level.

Economic indicators are generally published by international, national and regional public entities, particularly by Official Statistics Offices, although there exist also private entities such as banks or the NBER itself that also work on releasing some economic indicators. According to the Statistical Office of the European Union (Eurostat), the key economic indicators for the European Union area fall within the fields of national accounts, public finances, balance of payments, foreign trade, prices, monetary and financial accounts, and the labor market (Eurostat, 2011).

Some of the principal economic indicators include: the Gross Domestic Product (GDP), whose variations are generally used to measure economic growth; the Consumer Price Index (CPI), usually put in relation to inflation and that helps to measure the changes in the purchasing power of consumers;

the Industrial Production Index (IPI), which measures the evolution in the productive activity of a variety of industries; the Unemployment Rate, which is the number of unemployed people as a percentage of the labor force, and that is helpful to evaluate the overall status of the economy; or the External Trade Balance, calculated as a country exports minus imports, which measures the net income earned on international goods and services. A selection of the principal economic indicators have been briefly explained to provide some context, although there exist many other indicators, as reported by official bodies (Eurostat, 2011; OECD, 2018).

The indicators described above reflect macroeconomic magnitudes. Traditionally, these have been the most studied and reported given that they provide important information on the general status of a country economy and, at the same time, the tools available to obtain information (basically, surveys) were only able to provide aggregate figures. However, other type of indicators exist, as there are variety of activities that should be tracked to obtain the most complete understanding of an economic phenomena as possible. Especially important are microeconomic indicators, which are those that reflect magnitudes of particular interest for each industry. For instance, the indicator about arrivals at tourist accommodation establishments provides relevant information for the tourism sector.

Economic indicators are therefore of high relevance, as they help to monitor the evolution of the economy, having a central role to design and control public policies. The principal limitations of current economic indicators lie in the cost to produce them, the excessive level of aggregation of data and the delay in their publication. This causes a gap between the moment they are published and the moment in time they refer to, which frequently implies a late or insufficiently informed decision-making process (Bulligan et al., 2015).

In this context, the use of online data is particularly powerful, given that they do not only reflect social and economic behaviors, but also present some advantages, including: fast processing times because of their electronic nature; lower collection costs with respect to traditional tools such as surveys; and a higher level of granularity, as individual online movements can be tracked.

This makes it possible to generate fresh granular indicators, which are able to capture and reflect the particular behavior of an individual, firm or organization. These indicators could help in policy-making by complementing the information currently provided by official indicators. Moreover, they are particularly useful for firms, which could follow the concrete behavior of their customers, competitors or business segment. Online data are increasingly being used by marketing and data analytics companies, by academicians, and are also starting to be experimentally used by Statistics Offices and Central Banks, both for replicating current macroeconomic or microeconomic indicators and for producing alternative indicators.

1.1.4 Online-based Big Data to produce economic indicators

Statistics Offices, Central Banks and other official institutions are placing the Internet and the WWW as essential sources of social and economic information because they are generally updated and publicly accessible. These characteristics make online sources suitable to generate economic forecasts and build real-time indicators.

To mention some of the projects in this direction, the United Nations Economic Commission for Europe (UNECE) launched two projects, one in 2014 and another in 2015, focused on studying the role of Big Data in the modernization of the statistical production, along with the development of the "Sandbox" which consisted of an experimental environment to produce official statistics from online and other types of Big Data (UNECE, 2016).

Eurostat is doing some research activities focused on macroeconomic nowcasting and tourism forecasting with Big Data (Baldacci et al., 2016; Demunter, 2017) and on treating selectivity in Big Data sources for correctly employing them in official statistics (Beresewicz et al., 2018). Additionally, Eurostat was a coordinator of "ESSnet Big Data", a project within the European Statistical System (ESS) undertaken by 22 partners (generally, National Statistics Offices) from February 2016 to May 2018. Its main objective was integrating Big Data in the regular production of official statistics through the development of pilots to explore the potential of some Big Data sources (Debusschere, 2018). Eurostat has also collaborated with the academia and firms to explore the viability of producing demography, mobility and tourism statistics with Big Data (Seynaeve et al., 2016; Signorelli et al., 2017).

The Research Institute of the Finnish Economy (ETLA) publicly started to release results from the "ETLAnow" project in 2016, which continues in effect. This project has resulted in a promising economic forecasting tool that predicts the unemployment rate of each EU country three months ahead by using data retrieved from Google Trends and the latest official figures from Eurostat (Tuhkuri, 2016). Also related to unemployment, the Bank of Italy and the IZA Institute of Labor Economics conducted a research to assess the performance of an index of Google job-search intensity as a leading indicator for forecasting the monthly US unemployment rate (D'Amuri and Marcucci, 2017). Results showed that the majority of forecasting models that adopted the Google index outperformed the rest of models.

Similar conclusions were found by the Bank of Spain in collaboration with the University of Salamanca and the University of Amsterdam, that studied the viability of forecasting tourism inflows to Spain coming from Germany, United Kingdom (UK) and France by using Google Trends data that measured the relative popularity of some keywords related to traveling to Spain (Artola et al., 2015). The Federal Reserve Bank of New York in collaboration with Stanford University have also been actively working on economic forecasting with Big Data. They have recently published a work reviewing in which way methods to track economic conditions with Big Data and techniques to analyze such data have evolved over time, and how they are implemented by this bank to produce early estimates of GDP growth (Bok et al., 2018). From this brief overview it can be seen that the increasing interest in producing online-based economic indicators have strengthened the collaboration between official institutions and the academia, which is a positive effect.

One of the most important and worldwide known projects originated in the academia is "The Billion Prices Project", started by researchers of the MIT in 2008 and that continues running nowadays. This project is aimed at massively collecting retail prices posted online on the websites of retailers (by year 2010, they were collecting 5 million prices daily from over 300 retailers in 50 countries) and using these new source of digitized, fresh information about prices to improve the computation of traditional economic indicators, starting with the Consumer Price Index (CPI). The dynamics of online prices, their advantages and disadvantages and their viability as a reliable source of data for economic research have been studied too. Results show that the computed online price indexes co-move with consumer price indexes in most countries (Cavallo and Rigobon, 2016).

Another noteworthy case is that of the University of Warwick, that counts with the Data Science Lab, a research group focused on exploring and using data from online sources for detecting relationships between these data from the online world and social and economic processes occurring in the real world. For instance, they have found that changes in the volumes of queries done in Google for finance-related search terms act as early indicators of stock market moves (Preis et al., 2013), while for forecasting international tourism flows to the UK, data extracted from Wikipedia and Flickr have been successful (Alis et al., 2015; Barchiesi et al., 2015).

The unprecedented power of online sources to track social and economic phenomena has also attracted the interest of firms. For instance, it is possible to obtain valuable forecasts about the evolution of a business sector, information which is basic for decision-making and strategic management. According to the McKinsey Global Institute (2016), the potential impact of data analytics and Big Data was impressive in 2011, measured as a future increase of up to 60% in net income in the EU and US retail sectors or up to 50% lower production costs in the manufacturing sector (among many other examples available). However, as reported in year 2016, this potential impact is still potential, given that just some part of the value offered by Big Data has been captured up to date. For these reasons, the number of firms demanding Big Data analytics or implementing them within their processes, as well as the number of firms devoted to data science with the objective to offer valuable information for other firms or institutions has been increasing in the last years.

For these reasons, this **book** falls within a field whose relevance at an international level is increasing, and that is called to be crucial for the improvement of economic official statistics, policies, research and business management.

1.2 Motivation

In the Digital Era, with the increasing use of the Internet and digital devices, the way of interacting in the economic and social framework is completely transforming. Myriad individuals, companies and public organizations generate tons of data on a daily basis through the Internet. These online activities produce a digital footprint that can be tracked and, if treated with the proper systems and methods, could help to describe their behavior and, thus, to monitor key economic and social changes and trends. However, most research efforts performed with online data up to date have been focused on forecasting macroeconomic indicators, leaving the particular reality of firms almost forgotten and the granularity of online data unused.

The lack of research in generating real-time online-based economic indicators about concrete business aspects, along with the potential of online sources to capture the particular behavior and activities of firms have motivated the realization of this **book**. Our aim is to generate indicators capable to provide regularly updated and granular information about business activities for which this type is information is not currently available, and that is expected to help in making more informed decisions to policy-makers as well as business managers. To generate such indicators, nowcasting models have been used. The term "nowcasting", which is relatively recent, means "predicting the present"; that is, predicting the current, very near future of very recent past value of a variable.

Therefore, this **book** proposes to explore the possibility of generating online-based economic indicators about some business activities and characteristics. The economic topics for which we have designed online-based indicators have been selected because of their importance in the growth and modernization of the Spanish economy and their relevance for policy-making. Concretely, three online-based economic indicators have been designed and evaluated: the first is a predictor of a firm's export orientation, that is, a model that uses as input some online variables and with these data predicts whether a firm is engaged in exports; the second is a predictor of a firm's engagement in e-commerce, that is, a predictive model that using massive online data predicts if a firm is enrolled in electronic commerce (e-commerce); while the last one is a predictor of a firm's survival, which in short is composed by a predictive model whose output is a prediction about the status (dead or alive) of a firm, and by a model that provides its hazard rate.

From the wide range of Big Data sources available, the Internet and more particularly, the WWW, has been selected for the research conducted in this book. Its advantages and potential for economic forecasting are numerous, including: a strong relationship with economic phenomena, given that all agents participants in the economy are potential users of the Internet for a wide range of activities that leave a footprint of their intentions, actions and plans; the possibility to track this digital footprint (completely or partially) given that most of the data in websites are publicly available; fast processing times because of their electronic nature, taking advantage of the enormous advances in computation of the last years; lower collection costs with respect to traditional tools such as surveys, which have a high cost because of the human resources and processing times involved; and a higher level of granularity, given that individual online data can be tracked with the current technology.

Additionally, the publicly available nature of the WWW, the fact that corporate websites can be considered as the official images of firms on the Internet and their potential to reflect business activities and intentions, along with the technology which was available for this research that consisted in a proprietary web-scraping system, made this source the most appropriate. For these reasons, the indicators developed in this book are frequently referred to in the document as "web-based economic indicators".

1.3 Hypotheses and objectives

The purpose of this PhD book is to contribute to the research on producing up-to-date economic indicators with data retrieved, processed and analyzed from online sources, concretely from corporate websites, by employing a Big Data architecture and data analytics. Therefore, the general objective of this book is to design economic indicators based on data automatically retrieved from the WWW and to evaluate their performance with respect to the real values of the economic variables studied. The economic topics selected, as mentioned in the previous section, are firm's export orientation, firms' en-gagement in e-commerce and firm's survival.

The hypotheses formulated in this book are the following:

- **Hypothesis 1**: Data retrieved from corporate websites are able to reflect the export orientation of firms.

- **Hypothesis 2**: Data retrieved from corporate websites are able to reflect the engagement of firms in e-commerce.

- **Hypothesis 3**: Data retrieved from corporate websites are able to reflect the survival of firms.

The particular objectives to achieve, related to the formulated hypotheses and the general purpose of the book, include:

- **Objective 0**: Perform a state-of-the-art review of the literature about the principal Big Data sources, methods and applications in social and economic analyses.

- **Objective 1**: Design a web-based indicator of firms' export orientation and evaluate its performance.

- **Objective 2**: Design a web-based indicator of firms' engagement in e-commerce and evaluate its performance.

- **Objective 3**: Design a web-based indicator of firms' survival and evaluate its performance.

1.4 Structure of the book

This book is structured in six chapters, including this introductory chapter. The next four chapters correspond to the adaptation of four research papers published in different international scientific journals, while the last chapter is devoted to the conclusions. The overview of the book is as follows:

Chapter 2 presents the research paper entitled "Big Data sources and methods for social and economic analyses"[1], published in the scientific journal *Technological Forecasting and Social Change* which is indexed in the first quartile of Journal Citation Reports (JCR). This paper first reviews the new, digitized sources of social and economic data as well as the methods for processing such kind of data that are being used and proposed in the literature, with an important focus on nowcasting and forecasting purposes; second, it reviews the existing data lifecycle models and proposes a new one specifically focused on working with Big Data; third, and grounded on the previously proposed data lifecycle, it proposes an architecture for a Big Data system designed to combine data originating from different sources and process them with a variety of methods in order to forecast economic and social indicators. Therefore, it constitutes the theoretical framework of this book, and addresses Objective 0 of this book.

Chapter 3 presents the research paper entitled "Web data mining for monitoring business export orientation"[2], published in the scientific journal *Technological and Economic Development of Economy* which is indexed in the first quartile of JCR. This paper studies the viability of detecting and monitoring the export orientation of firms by using web-based variables automatically retrieved and processed. To download and analyze the online information, part of the Big Data system described in Chapter 2 was implemented. This research evidences that web-based variables are able to predict firm export orientation

---

[1]Research paper published in the scientific journal *Technological Forecasting and Social Change*, in volume 130 of May 2018, pages 99-113, with DOI 10.1016/j.techfore.2017.07.027.

[2]Research paper published in the scientific journal *Technological and Economic Development of Economy*, in volume 24, issue 2 of March 2018, pages 406-428, with DOI 10.3846/20294913.2016.1213193.

with a high accuracy, which is not significantly diminished when the process of retrieving and analyzing such variables is automated. Therefore, this paper addresses Objective 1 of this book.

Chapter 4 presents the research paper entitled "Monitoring e-commerce adoption from online data"[3], published in the scientific journal *Knowledge and Information Systems* which is indexed in the second quartile of JCR. This paper evaluates the viability of detecting and monitoring the engagement in e-commerce of firms by using online data automatically retrieved and processed from their corporate websites. To download and analyze the online information, we departed from the partial implementation of the Big Data system explained in Chapter 3 and expanded it with additional functionalities. Results of this research showed that automatic web-based variables are also able to predict firms' enrollment in e-commerce with a high level of accuracy. Therefore, this paper covers Objective 2 of this book.

Chapter 5 presents the research paper entitled "Do corporate websites' changes reflect firms' survival?"[4], published in the scientific journal *Online Information Review* which is indexed in the second quartile of JCR. This paper studies the relationship between the status of corporate websites (down, unchanged or updated) and the status of firms (active or inactive). It verifies that changes in the contents of corporate websites are clearly related to the firms' status, revealing a new source for business demography monitoring. Therefore, this paper addresses Objective 3 of this book.

Finally, Chapter 6 summarizes the contributions of this book, explains its implications and establishes its limitations and lines of future work.

Synthetically, the objectives, hypotheses and structure of this book are shown in Figure 1.1

---

[3]Research paper published online on June 2018 in the scientific journal *Knowledge and Information Systems*, with DOI 10.1007/s10115-018-1233-7.

[4]Research paper published in the scientific journal *Online Information Review*, in Volume 42, issue 6 of year 2018, pages 956-970, with DOI 10.1108/OIR-11-2016-0321.

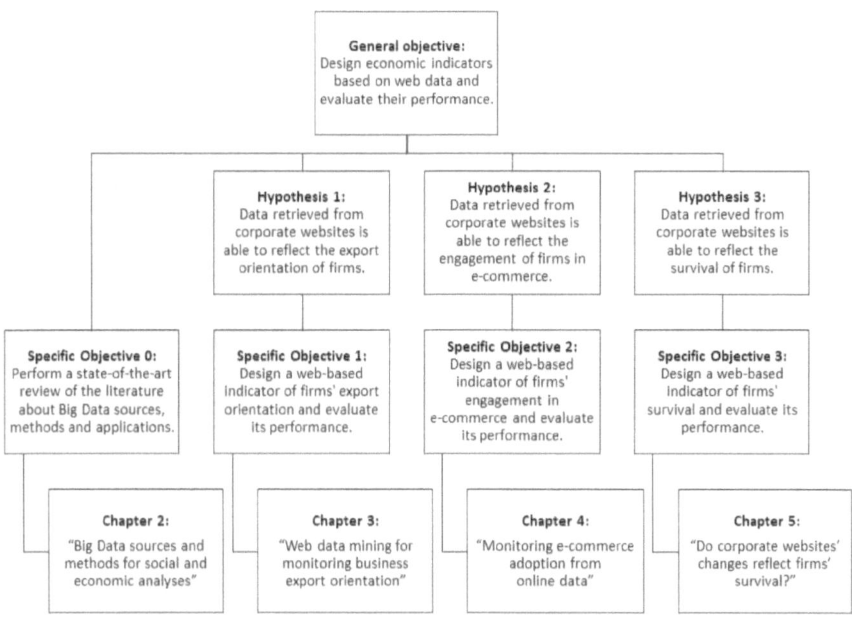

Figure 1.1: Objectives, hypotheses and structure of the book

Chapter 2

Big Data sources and methods for social and economic analyses

Chapter 2 is an adapted version of this published research paper:

- Title: Big Data sources and methods for social and economic analyses
- Authors: Desamparados Blazquez and Josep Domenech
- Year of publication: 2018
- Journal: Technological Forecasting and Social Change
- Volume: 130
- Pages: 99-113
- DOI: 10.1016/j.techfore.2017.07.027

2.1 Introduction

What comes to your mind when talking about "The Digital Era"? For sure,
concepts as the "Internet", "Smartphones" or "Smart sensors" arise. These
technologies are progressively being used in most of the everyday activities of
companies and individuals. For instance, many companies conduct mar-keting
campaigns through social networks, sell their products online, monitor the
routes followed by sales representatives with smartphones or register the
performance of machinery with specific sensors. At the other side, individuals
make use of computers, smartphones and tablets in order to buy products
online, share their opinions, chat with friends or check the way to some place.
Moreover, citizens' movements and activities are daily registered by sensors
placed in any part of cities or roads and in public places such as supermarkets.
Therefore, all of these technologies are generating tons of digitized and fresh
data about people and firms' activities that properly analyzed, could help reveal
trends and monitor economic, industrial and social behaviors or magnitudes.
These data are not only updated, but also massive, given that daily data
generation has been recently estimated in 2.5 Exabytes (IBM, 2016).

For this reason, they are commonly referred to as "Big Data", concept which first appeared in the late 90s (Cox and Ellsworth, 1997) and was defined in the early 2000s in terms of the 3Vs model (Laney, 2001), which refers to: Volume (size of data), Velocity (speed of data transfers), and Variety (different types of data, ranging from video to data logs for instance, and with different structures). This model evolved to adapt to the changing digital reality, so that it was extended to 4Vs, adding the "Value" dimension (process to extract valuable information from data, known as Big Data Analytics). Currently, the "Big Data" concept is starting to be defined in terms of the 5Vs model (Bello-Orgaz et al., 2016), which added the "Veracity" dimension (related to proper data governance and privacy concerns).

This new data paradigm is called to transform the landscape for socio-economic policy and research (Einav and Levin, 2014; Varian, 2014) as well as for business management and decision-making. Thus, identifying which data sources are available, what type of data they provide, and how to treat these data is basic to generate as much value as possible for the company or organization. In this context, a Big Data architecture adapted to the specific domain and purpose of the organization contributes to systematize the process of generating value. This architecture should be capable of managing the complete data lifecycle in the organization, including data ingestion, analysis and storage, among others.

Furthermore, the design of a Big Data architecture should consider the numerous challenges that this paradigm implies. These include: scalability, data availability, data integrity, data transformation, data quality, data provenance (related to generation of right metadata that identify the origin of data as well as the processes applied to them during the data lifecycle, to assure traceability), management of huge volumes of information, data heterogeneity (structured and unstructured, with different time frequencies), integration of data from different sources, data matching, bias, availability of tools for properly analyzing such kind of data, processing complexity, privacy and legal issues, and data governance (Fan et al., 2014; Jagadish et al., 2014; Hashem et al., 2015).

The Big Data paradigm also offers many advantages and benefits for the companies, governments, and the society. Jin et al. (2015) highlight its potential contribution to national and industrial development, as it enforces to change and upgrade research methods, promotes and makes it easy to conduct interdisciplinary research, helps to nowcast the present and to forecast the future more precisely. In this vein, first big data architectures designed for specific fields are being proposed in order to surpass the previously mentioned challenges and make the most of the data available with the aim of nowcasting and forecasting variables of interest.

However, no specific architecture for social and economic forecasting has been proposed yet. This emerges as a necessity, in the one hand, because of the particular nature of socio-economic data, which have important components of uncertainty and human behavior that are particularly complex to model; and, in the other hand, because of the great benefits that can be derived from the use of big data to forecast economic and social change. For instance, big data approaches have been proved to improve predictions of economic indicators such as the unemployment level (Vicente et al., 2015), help managers detect market trends so that they can anticipate opportunities, and also help policy-makers monitor faster and more precisely the effects of a wide range of policies and public grants (Blazquez and Domenech, 2018b).

In this context, this paper aims to i) establish a framework about the new and potentially useful available sources of socio-economic data and new methods devoted to deal with these data, ii) propose a new data lifecycle model that encompasses all the processes related to working with big data, and iii) propose an architecture for a Big Data system able to integrate, process and analyze data from different sources with the objective to forecast economic and social change.

The remainder of the paper is organized as follows: Section 2.2 reviews the big data architectures proposed in the literature; Section 2.3 compiles the new socio-economic data sources emerged in the digital era and proposes a classification of them; Section 2.4 reviews the new methods and analytics designed to deal with big data and establishes a taxonomy of these methods; Section

2.5 depicts the data lifecycle on which the proposed Big Data architecture is based; Section 2.6 proposes a Big Data architecture for nowcasting social and economic variables, explaining its different modules; finally, Section 2.7 draws some concluding remarks.

2.2 Related work

Since the advent of the concept of "Big Data" two decades ago, some architectures to manage and analyze such data in different fields have been proposed, having their technical roots in distributed computing paradigms such as grid computing (Berman et al., 2003). However, the current data explosion also referred to as "Data Big Bang"(Pesenson et al., 2010) in which there is a daily generation of vast quantities of data from a variety of formats and sources, is revealing the fullest meaning of "Big Data".

The particular properties and challenges that the current big data context opens require specific architectures for information systems particularly designed to retrieve, process, analyze and store such volume and variety of data. Therefore, we are living the constant births of new technologies conceived to be useful in this context such as, to mention some, cloud and exascale computing (Bahrami and Singhal, 2014; Reed and Dongarra, 2015). Given this recent technological and data revolution, research in this topic is in its early stage (Chen et al., 2014). In this section, we review the novel and incipient research works that develop general frameworks and specific architectures for adopting the Big Data approach in different fields from the point of view of data analytics applications.

Pääkkönen and Pakkala (2015) proposed a reference architecture for Big Data systems based on the analysis of some implementation cases. This work describes a number of functionalities expected to be considered when designing a Big Data architecture for a specific knowledge field, business or industrial process. These include: Data sources, data extraction, data loading and preprocessing, data processing, data analysis, data transformation, interfacing and visualization, data storage and model specification. Besides that, Assunção et al. (2015) reflected on some components that should be present in any Big Data architecture by depicting the four most common phases within a Big Data analytics workflow: Data sources, data management (including tasks such as preprocessing or filtering), modelling, and result analysis and visualization. This scheme was put in relation to cloud computing, whose potential and benefits for storing huge amounts of data and performing powerful calculus are positioning it as a desirable technology to be included in the design of a Big Data architecture. Concretely, the role of cloud computing as part of a Big Data system has been explored by Hashem et al. (2015).

About architectures for specific domains, Zhang et al. (2017) proposed a Big Data analytics architecture with the aim of exploiting industrial data to achieve cleaner production processes and optimize the product lifecycle management. This architecture works in four main stages: in stage 1, services of product lifecycle management, such as design improvement, are applied; in stage 2 the architecture acquires and integrates big data from different industrial sources, such as sensors; in stage 3, big data is processed and stored depending on their structure; finally, in stage 4 big data mining and knowledge discovery is conducted by means of four layers: the data layer (mixing data), the method layer (data extraction), the result layer (data mining) and the application layer (meeting the demands of the enterprise). Results from last stage fill the ERP systems and are used along with decision support systems to improve product-related services and give feedback in all product lifecycle stages.

In the domain of healthcare, a complete and specific Big Data analytics architecture was developed by Wang et al. (2016a). This architecture was based on the experiences about best practices in implementing Big Data systems in the industry, and was composed of five major layers: first, the data layer, which includes the data sources to be used for supporting operations and problem solving; second, the data aggregation layer, which is in charge of acquiring, transforming and storing data; third, the analytics layer, which is in charge of processing and analyzing data; fourth, the information exploration layer, which works by generating outputs for clinical decision support, such as real-time monitoring of potential medical risks; last, the data governance layer, which is in charge of managing business data throughout its entire life-cycle by applying the proper standards and policies of security and privacy. This layer is particularly necessary in this case given the sensibility of clinical data.

The review of these architectures evidenced some common modules or functionalities. After homogenizing the different names for modules very similar responsibilities, and considering their sequence in the process, they can be summarized as follows: first, a data module, which includes different sources of data with different formats; second, a data preprocessing module, which includes data extraction, integration and transformation; third, a data analytics module, which includes modelling and analysis techniques for knowledge discovery; and fourth, a results and visualization module, which includes tools for representing the results in a way useful for the firm or organization.

However, there are other functionalities whose location within the Big Data architecture is not homogeneous across the different proposals. For instance, the data storage responsibilities, which are basic for enabling data reuse and bringing access to previous results, have been included in a variety of places, ranging from being included in the data module (Assunção et al., 2015) or the preprocessing module (Wang et al., 2016a; Zhang et al., 2017), to being a macro-functionality present in each module of the architecture (Pääkkönen and Pakkala, 2015). The last approach is better reflecting the nature and complexity of big data analysis, given that not only the original data requires storage, but also the integrated data, processed data, and the results derived from data analytics.

Other functionalities whose consideration in the literature has been divergent are those related to data governance, which is concerned to preserve privacy, security and assure the accomplishment of data-related regulations. Despite its importance, data governance was only considered by Wang et al. (2016a). As long as the 5Vs model expands, data governance is expected to gain relevance and become a requirement in the design of any Big Data architecture.

For the case of Big Data for social or economic domains, no specific architecture has been proposed yet in the literature. Given their particular characteristics and increasing potential for detecting and monitoring behaviors and trends, which is basic to anticipate events, design better action plans and make more informed decisions, an architecture specifically devoted to treat these data emerges as necessary. Thus, this work proposes a Big Data architecture designed for nowcasting and forecasting social and economic change. This proposal aims to help business implement the most appropriate architecture for their decision making needs, make the most of the data available and assure that it is treated according to the ethic and legal standards.

2.3 Non-traditional sources of social and economic data

The digital footprint left by individuals has caused an exponential growth of the data sources available for social and economic analyses, which broadens the possibilities for conducting socio-economic studies beyond traditional data sources, namely surveys and official records. Although the reasons why these new data are generated are numerous, the way they are generated has important ethical and legal implications. For instance, personal data in a purchase order cannot be used for the same purposes as the data from a public profile in Twitter. To some extent, the usage of the data is limited by how they are generated. This fact motivated us to review and classify the newborn non-traditional sources of social and economic data according to the purpose of the user generating the data, as Figure 2.1 shows.

The first level in the taxonomy includes five categories: i) purpose of searching for information; ii) purpose of conducting a transaction, that could be of a financial or non-financial nature; iii) purpose of disseminating information; iv) purpose of doing a social interaction; and v) not a deliberate purpose. The first four categories correspond to an active generation of data, while the last correspond to an inactive generation: that is, data is not intentionally gen-

erated as a result of a particular purpose, but just derived from the own use
of any device (PC, smartphone, tablet...) with any of the purposes explained
above. Data that fall in this category have been divided in three types: usage
data, location data and personal data. A brief description of each purpose
from which data is generated and examples of sources involved in each data
generation process is shown in Table 2.1.

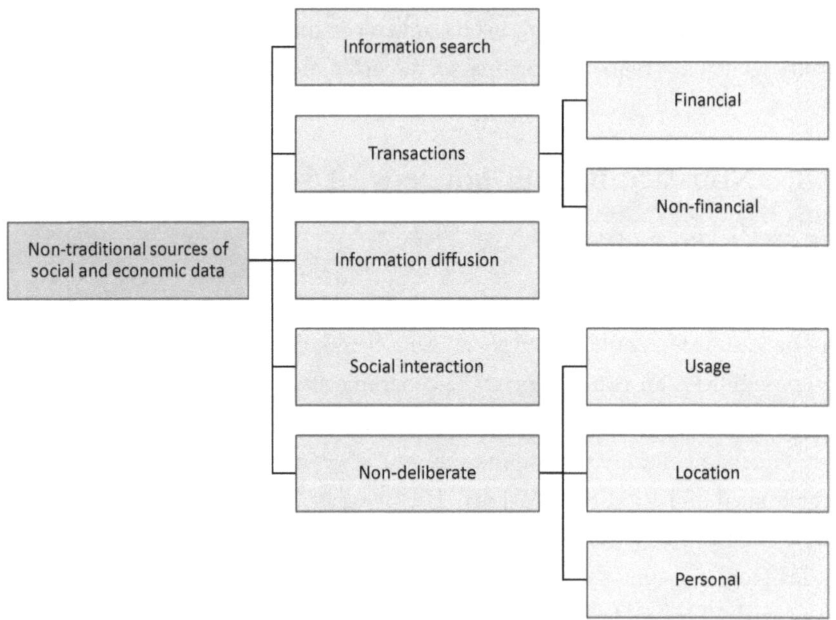

Figure 2.1: Taxonomy of non-traditional sources of social and economic data

The majority of non-traditional sources of social and economic mentioned
above needs the Internet for working. Indeed, the increasing penetration and
importance of the Internet in almost every social and economic activity has
positioned it as a basic means for the generation of such kind of data.

Table 2.1: Classification of sources of socio-economic Big Data

User's purpose	*Description*	*Examples of sources*
Information search	The user aims to find information about a topic of his interest. Data is actively generated	Search engines, Google Trends
Transactions	The user interacts with an individual and/or machine to achieve an agreement in which the user demands and obtains a product or service in exchange for a financial or non-financial compensation. Data is actively generated	
• Financial transactions	Event in which the user makes a payment to obtain a product or service	E-banking, e-commerce, urban sensors (tolls, credit card readers, retail scanners, public transport card readers)
• Non-financial transactions	Event in which the user provides the counterpart with required information to obtain a product or service	E-government, e-recruiting
Information diffusion	The user aims to spread information or knowledge. This includes marketing purposes, in order to establish a public image of the user or the agent he represents. Data is actively generated	Corporate websites, Apps, Wiki pages
Social interaction	The user wants to share information, opinions and ideas with other users. Data is actively generated	Social networking sites, opinion platforms, blogs
Non-deliberate	The user does not pursue to generate data with his/her action, but data are generated by the use of some means. Data is passively generated as a result of any other user action	
• Usage	The simple fact of using any device generates data related to how, when and where an action has been done	Web cookies, Internet Protocol, Sensors for self-tracking
• Location	The use of mobile phones generates data particularly related to the position of the user	GPS, GSM, Call Detail Records, Bluetooth, WiFi Points
• Personal	Personal data (age, sex, etc.) is generated consciously (e.g. filling a form to complete a purchase) or unconsciously (e.g. data about the type of information we look for is used to infer our incomes) as a consequence of using any device or tool to achieve a purpose	Forms, profiles, type of searches or purchases

2.3.1 The Internet as basic means for generating socio-economic data

The "Data Big Bang" originated in the Internet, which unstoppable expands, is transforming the way of interacting in the economic and social framework. Myriad individuals, companies and public organizations search, post and generate tons of information daily through the Internet. These online activities leave behind a digital footprint that can be tracked and, if treated with the proper Big Data architecture, could help to describe their behavior, decisions and intentions, and thus, to monitor key economic and social changes and trends. Indeed, recent research highlighted the increasing role of the Internet as a provider of data for explaining, modelling, nowcasting and forecasting social behaviors (Askitas and Zimmermann, 2015).

2.3.1.1 Google Trends: the power of search engines

Google Trends (GT) is an Internet-based facility, released on May 2006, which provides up-to-date reports on the volume of search queries on a specific keyword or text, with historic searches available since January 2004. It captures how the demand of information under certain topics varies over time, providing useful data to detect emerging trends and underlying interests and concerns of society. The use of GT data to nowcast social and economic (particularly macroeconomic) variables was introduced by Choi and Varian (2009b,a), who showed that some search categories in the Google search engine helped to predict car and home sales, incoming tourists or unemployment claims. Afterwards, various studies in different countries focused on improving unemployment-related variables' forecasts by using GT data, obtaining successful results (Askitas and Zimmermann, 2009; McLaren and Shanbhogue, 2011; Fondeur and Karamé, 2013; Vicente et al., 2015).

The aggregate consumer behavior in different sectors has also been successfully predicted with GT data. For instance, using GT data as predictors has been proved to improve forecasts of tourist inflows (Artola et al., 2015; Bangwayo-Skeete and Skeete, 2015), of trading decisions and transaction vol-

umes on the stock market (Preis et al., 2013; Moat et al., 2014), of private
purchases of different goods and services (Vosen and Schmidt, 2011) or of cin-
ema admissions (Hand and Judge, 2012). Recently, GT data have proven to
be useful for forecasting political inquiries' results (Mavragani and Tsagarakis,
2016). However, elections results and topics with such components of opinion
and ideology have been particularly studied through data from sites focused
on social interaction, as are Social Networking Sites (SNS) such as Facebook
or Twitter and opinion platforms such as Ciao.

2.3.1.2   Social Networking Sites and blogs

SNS are online places specifically addressed to encourage users express their
feelings and opinions about any kind of topic. Therefore, the information they
contain is to some extent a reflection of what happens in society. Indeed, the
term "Social Big Data" is becoming popular to refer to data generated by
SNS and blogs (Bello-Orgaz et al., 2016). For that reason more attention is
being paid to SNS as sources of data potentially useful in forecasting social
variables.

Among SNS, the microblogging service Twitter is one of the most popular,
with 332 million users who are active monthly and send on average more than
500 million tweets per day. This huge amount of "user-generated" information,
though implies some issues, weaknesses and challenges that require further
research (Gayo-Avello, 2013; Schoen et al., 2013), could help to predict both
present and future social and economic events, as verified in different works.
For instance, tweets' contents have helped to describe political preferences
and forecast elections results (Tumasjan et al., 2011; Kim and Park, 2012;
Ceron et al., 2014), to predict stock market movements (Bollen et al., 2011),
to forecast box office in the motion pictures industry (Kim et al., 2015; Gaikar
et al., 2015) or to monitor the public opinion on new policies (Ceron and Negri,
2016).

Facebook, which is the third most visited site worldwide[1] with 1,650 millions of active users, doubtlessly also represents a source of powerful data for analyzing social and economic behaviors. However, given that its contents are more heterogeneous and user-adjustable, they are also more difficult to retrieve and analyze. Notwithstanding this, incipient studies have shown the ability of Facebook data to determine consuming profiles, which are useful for marketing purposes (Arrigo et al., 2016), and to predict election results and the population's political orientation (Cameron et al., 2016; David et al., 2016).

Other principal SNS are LinkedIn, Youtube, Instagram, Google+, Tumblr and Flickr (Bello-Orgaz et al., 2016). They are also rich sources of social and economic data, which could eventually be used to find changes in the unemployment patterns or detect what entertainment activities people prefer, among other topics (Russell, 2013). However, the diverse and complex formats of the information provided, along with the newness in some of these SNS, makes them remained almost unexplored. It should be noted that blogs are also important generators of "Social Big Data", though research in relating blogs' data to forecasting is also in its early stage. The pioneer work of Liu et al. (2007) examined the usefulness of opinions and sentiments extracted from blogs to forecast sales performance, while more recently Saleiro et al. (2015) combined data from news, blogs and SNS to track political opinion in real time. Nevertheless, these sources are not without limitations. It is common that they are biased towards one segment of the population, e.g., young people, or English language, e.g., blogs in non-English language links more frequently English content than the other way round (Thelwall, 2007). Thus, some correcting measures should be considered before generalization (Gayo-Avello, 2012).

---

[1] alexa.com

2.3.1.3   Websites and Apps: transactional, opinion platforms and information diffusion

In the Digital Era, firms generally establish their official public image on the Internet by implementing corporate websites. Through these sites, companies inform about their products, services, organizational structure and intentions, such as exporting or opening a branch office abroad. Corporate websites encompass all kind of websites implemented by firms in relation to their economic activity, ranging from websites used only to give information about the firm, to transactional websites devoted not only to provide information but also to offer online services (e-commerce, e-banking...), about which users are sometimes allowed to give their opinion in the website itself. That is, corporate websites may present three different functionalities: spreading information about firms (related to establishing a public image), conducting transactions (e-business processes) and facilitating opinion sharing (electronic word-of-mouth (eWOM) booster).

It is remarkable that websites have a complex structure which differ from one case to another, so that standardizing the retrieval and analysis of their information requires from a specific big data architecture. That difficulty has contributed to corporate websites being an almost unexplored source of data. However, their public, updated and "business generated" nature makes them potential sources of economic data. Moreover, business characteristics could emerge on the web and be monitored by massively analyzing corporate websites, as recent research shows.

Applying big data approaches (particularly web data mining and machine learning) to the "spreading information" functionality of corporate websites, firms' sales growth and business activities such as strategies of technology adoption, innovation and R&D have been successfully detected (Arora et al., 2013, 2016; Gök et al., 2015; Li et al., 2016). In addition, by using a specifically designed web data mining system for analyzing corporate websites (Domenech et al., 2012) the export orientation of firms has also been successfully detected (Blazquez and Domenech, 2018b). In addition, there exist other type of websites created with the specific aim of spreading information, such as are Wiki pages, from which Wikipedia is the most important representative nowadays with more than 730 million unique visitors monthly (Wikimedia Foundation, 2017). Its penetration in the society along with its collaborative nature have positioned it as a potential source of social and behavioral data. Concretely, Wikipedia page views, edits and contents have already proven to be useful for socio-economic forecasting. Incipient research works have successfully used Wikipedia data to better forecast stock market movements (Moat et al., 2014) and tourism demand (Alis et al., 2015; Khadivi and Ramakrishnan, 2016). This kind of studies aim to create new indicators in advance or to complement those used in current official statistics.

The prominent role of the Internet in today's economy and society has promoted the emergence of e-business services, which firms can use to sell their products and do transactions in an online base with customers (E-Commerce), recruit candidates (E-Recruiting) or offer their services online (e.g. E-banking). E-Business may even go a step further and represent not only a complementary tool for firms (e.g., selling locally and online), but a new type of business model characterized by operating just online. Many of these sites offer users the chance to post their opinions and do reviews on the product or service acquired, which may range from any manufacture to a hotel stay or an experience in a restaurant. This web feature is generally known as opinion platform (even a website can be designed just to act as opinion platform), which is used to bring together online communities of users, whose opinions are basic information for social science research.

One of the most important e-commerce and opinion platform worldwide is Amazon. It is one of the biggest online retailers, with more than 300 million active customers' accounts. This website provides customers' reviews and opinions on millions of products and services, being therefore a source of data potentially useful to detect consumer preferences or predict sales. For instance, the forecast of consumer product demands in Amazon.com has been significantly improved by using the textual contents of consumer reviews (Chong et al., 2015; Schneider and Gupta, 2016). Another noteworthy topic

for managers is to detect the so-called "influencers" in consumer-opinion platforms, given that their comments may influence other consumers' purchase
behavior and, thus, detecting and monitoring them is essential. For instance,
Arenas-Márquez et al. (2014) successfully identified influencers in Ciao.com
by retrieving and analyzing characteristics of the product reviews such as the
rating received by other users.

Other sites that provide potentially useful data for detecting social and economic trends are, for instance, eBay.com, whose information has been helpful to explain price differences among remanufactured, used and new items
(Frota Neto et al., 2016), TripAdvisor.com, which has been successfully used
to detect tourist preferences thus helping hotel managers to adapt their offers
(Li et al., 2015), or Monster.com, that organizes the available job offers and
helps to track changes in job search (Edelman, 2012).

When using opinion platforms as sources for social and economic analyses,
limitations related to the veracity of the contents must be considered. Sellers
and marketers may have the temptation to generate fake consumer reviews
to influence in the consumer decision (Malbon, 2013). In this context, some
techniques for detecting such manipulations could be applied to alleviate this
limitation (Hu et al., 2012).

Apps provide access to information and services that may or may not be
offered by other means, such as websites. Since the use of apps is becoming widespread in the daily activities of individuals and organizations, they
have become a source of data with great potential for forecasting social and
economic topics. Although accessing data generated by them is currently a
difficult task, some incipient research works are appearing. To date, apps data
logs haven been proved to be successful for forecasting users' intentions to use a
specific app, automatically forecasting depression (Wang et al., 2016b; Suhara
et al., 2017) or helping to detect mobility patterns as reviewed by Pan and
Yang (2016).

2.3.2 Urban and mobile sensors

Ubiquitous computing is one of the technological areas that has experimented the greatest development in the context of the Digital Era. Its advances have resulted in the generation of wireless, inconspicuous and inexpensive sensors to gather information on our everyday life activities (Krishnan and Cook, 2014). Specifically, urban sensors and mobile embedded sensors are potential generators of social and economic data.

Among urban sensors, one of the most widespread and used worldwide is the credit card reader. Credit card transactions are recorded and provide data potentially useful for firms to detect and predict, for instance, personal bankruptcy (Xiong et al., 2013), fraudulent purchases in online stores (Van Vlasselaer et al., 2015) or default and repayment, which in the context of credit card companies is useful for defining marketing strategies (Einav and Levin, 2014).

Retail scanners are also very extended, and their function is to record the characteristics of customers' everyday purchases. These data has proven to be useful for forecasting consumer behaviors, sales and prices, as recent research shows. For instance, Dey et al. (2014) successfully used retail level scanner data to model market trends, prices and sales in the industry of catfish products, suggesting a particular competition strategy based on the results obtained. Another study, focused on explaining human behavior, employed weekly scanner data to detect consumer boycotts in response to an international conflict (Pandya and Venkatesan, 2016).

A pioneer study by Askitas and Zimmermann (2013) successfully used data from tolls to nowcast business cycles, creating a Toll Index that represent a technological, innovation-driven economic telemetry. Other sensor networks that provide useful data for forecasting a manifold of socio-economic variables are smart grid, WiFi access points or public transport card readers, among others (Kitchin, 2014; Chou and Ngo, 2016).

Some sensors embedded in mobile phones are also potential sources of social data: GSM, GPS, Bluetooth, accelerometer or sensors for connecting

to the telephonic network through Base Transceiver Stations (which produce
the so-called "Call Details Record", with information regarding all call-related
activities, such as sending SMS or phoning, conducted by mobile phone users
in the network). These sensors generate data related to the user location that
have been successfully used to study social behaviors, preferences and mobility
patterns. Properly treated, these data can contribute to better understand in
which way human mobility affects well-being and human behaviors at the
micro level, and social organization and change at the macro level (Williams
et al., 2015).

Concretely, data from such sensors have been useful for detecting places
of interest, that is, places where people go and stay for a while (Montoliu
et al., 2013), and for detecting personality traits, which companies may use
to personalize their services (Chittaranjan et al., 2013). Moreover, Laurila
et al. (2013) summarized different human behaviors analyzed to date with
such mobile embedded sensors data, including: mobility patterns and their
relation with the weather, the perceived level of safeness and intimacy of a
given location, the relation among moves from individuals and from their
friends and acquaintances, or the transition between spatial habitats. Other
recent applications of mobile phones' data in relation to mobility are recreating
and drawing maps of population distribution (Deville et al., 2014; Graells-
Garrido et al., 2016) and detecting anomalous behavioral patterns associated
to emergency (e.g. earthquakes) and non-emergency (e.g. holidays) events
(Dobra et al., 2015).

2.4 Non-traditional methods for processing social and economic data

Data obtained from non-traditional socio-economic sources are generally large,
heterogeneous and unstructured or semi-structured. These characteristics imply a number of challenges when it comes to retrieving, processing, analyzing
and storing data. Accordingly, methods and techniques related to machine

learning and Big Data are being developed. Many of such methods have been widely applied in other knowledge fields such as engineering, medicine or biostatistics. Despite their potential for treating socio-economic data, their application in this field is still at an early stage (Varian, 2014).

This section enumerates and describes the most relevant methods for treating socio-economic data from a Big Data approach, with the objective of providing a framework. The reviewed techniques are summarized and classified in a taxonomy illustrated in Figure 2.2.

2.4.1 Methods for structuring data

Big data sources can be classified as structured (tabular data), semi-structured (data with machine-readable tags that do not follow a strict standard) or unstructured (data that lacks from any scheme allowing machines to understand them, e.g. a video). Since analysis algorithms require some structure to interpret the data and given that about 95% of big data is unstructured (Gandomi and Haider, 2015), the process of structuring the information is basic. This includes transforming the data into an organized set, with clearly defined variables and the relations among them identified. Below, some of the most common methods for structuring data with applications to social and economic analysis are surveyed.

Almost any source of data, and particularly the Internet, is plenty of human generated text that requires proper retrieval and processing. To exploit the full potential of text in databases, specific techniques for processing natural language are required. Natural Language Processing (NLP) is a research area focused on exploring how computers can be used to understand and shape natural language text so that it can be useful for different applications (Chowdhury, 2005). NLP is in itself a computational method that comprehends a series of techniques that provide an easy interface for information retrieval systems and, at the same time, to structure texts in different ways so that the underlying information can be more easily extracted. Some interesting NLP techniques for social analysis are Sentiment Analysis (also referred to

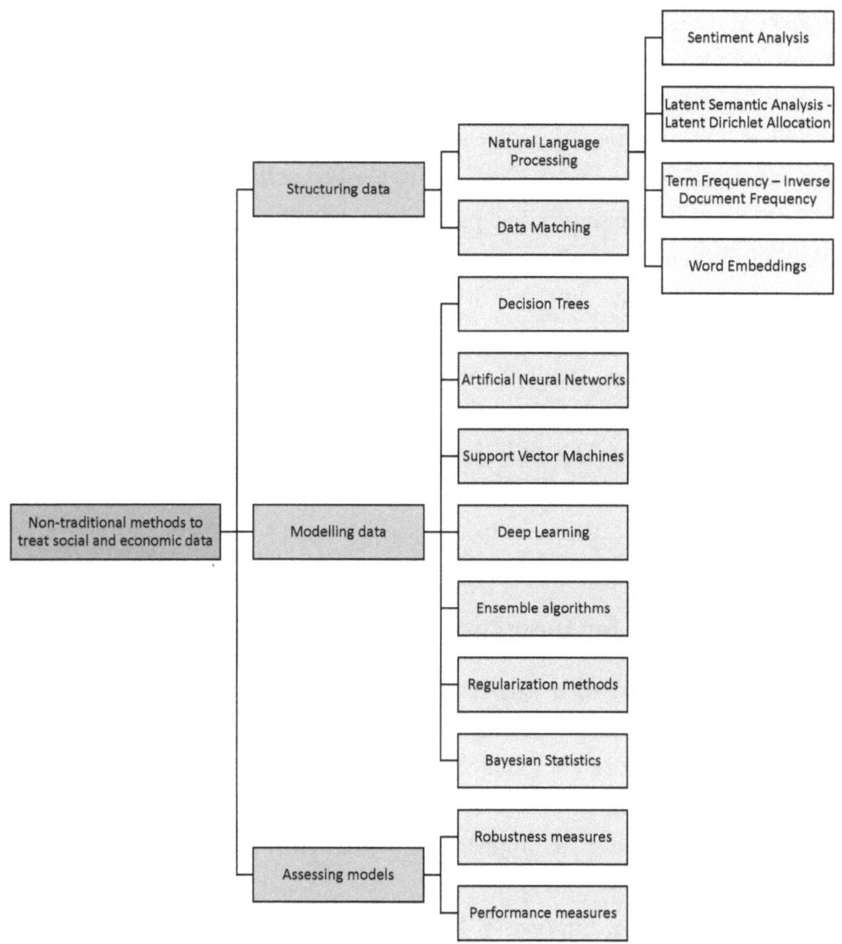

Figure 2.2: Taxonomy of non-traditional methods to treat social and economic data

as Opinion Mining), Latent Semantic Analysis (LSA), Latent Dirichlet Allocation (LDA), TF-IDF (Term Frequency - Inverse Document Frequency) and Word Embeddings. Liu (2012), Evangelopoulos et al. (2012), Blei et al. (2003),

Moro et al. (2015), Armentano et al. (2014) and Rudolph et al. (2016), among others, provide some reference for these methods.

Linking records from the same user (or entity) across different data sources is also an important challenge for analyzing social and economic information. Data Matching (which is also commonly known as Record Linkage or Entity Resolution) is a computational process used to identify, match and merge records from several databases that correspond to the same entities. A special case of data matching is deduplication, which consists in the identification and matching of records about the same entities within just one database (this step is crucial in data cleaning). Matched data are becoming more important because they may contain information impossible to obtain by means of other sources or processes. This technique is a complex process encompassing five steps, from data cleaning and standardization to data quality and completeness measuring. For a detailed description, see the work by Vatsalan et al. (2013).

2.4.2 Methods for modelling data

Modelling data (and their relationships) is the main process in a big data analysis. This includes reducing the dimensionality of data sets, applying modeling techniques to data and obtaining outcomes. Depending on the type of data available and the objective of the analysis, two different paradigms for modelling data may be applied: Supervised Learning and Unsupervised Learning (Hastie et al., 2013).

On the one hand, Supervised Learning refers to problems in which each observation in a data set has inputs (also referred to as independent variables, features or predictors) and outputs (also referred to as targets, responses or dependent variables), and the main goal is to use inputs in order to infer the values of outputs. These problems can be further categorized as classification problems, in which outputs are expressed as categories, or as regression problems, in which outputs are expressed in a continuous space. On the other hand, Unsupervised Learning refers to problems in which each observation has some inputs but no outputs, and the main goal is to find the relationships or structure among inputs. These problems can be further categorized into clustering problems, in which the goal is to discover groupings in the data, and association problems, in which the objective is to find rules that describe the behavior of part of the data.

Depending on the learning paradigm, different machine learning techniques can be applied. For nowcasting and forecasting applications, supervised methods are generally employed. The most common supervised machine learning techniques successfully applied in other disciplines, such as medicine or engineering, and that are potentially useful for the social sciences, are enumerated below.

Linear and logistic regression are two useful machine learning techniques widely applied by economists and social scientists. However, alternative methods to regressions have been developed and demonstrated to perform as well as or better when using big data sets (Varian, 2014). For instance, Decision Trees, which are a type of predictive models that can be used to represent both classifiers and regression models; Support Vector Network (Cortes and Vapnik, 1995), more commonly known as Support Vector Machine (SVM), which is a learning machine for two-group classification; Artificial Neural Networks (ANN), which are two-stage regression or classification models able to identify non-linear relations among a set of input variables, and generate forecasts about the variable under study by modelling and weighting those relations (Hastie et al., 2013); or Deep Learning methods, which develop a layered and hierarchical architecture where higher-level (more abstract) features are obtained by transforming lower-level (less abstract) features. For classification, higher-level features highlight aspects of the raw input that are relevant for discrimination. Deep Learning methods can deal with huge quantities of unstructured data, reason why they are positioning as a promising tool in Big Data Analysis (LeCun et al., 2015; Najafabadi et al., 2015). ANN and Deep Learning are special cases, given that their learning algorithms can be either supervised or unsupervised.

In addition, there exist a group of techniques which are focused on improving the performance of the previously described ones, and that are starting to be known as "Ensemble algorithms". Some of these algorithms work by adding randomness to data, which is a useful procedure to deal with overfitting. These techniques include the Bootstrap, Bagging, Boosting and Random Forests (Varian, 2014).

Regularization methods are another group of supervised learning techniques, whose objective is to obtain sparse solutions and that, due to the increased amount of information available, have been increasingly studied in recent years by the scientific community (Friedman et al., 2010). These methods can be applied to a number of supervised learning techniques, from regressions to support vector machines, and include, to mention some examples: the Least Absolute Shrinkage and Selection Operator (LASSO), which was one of the first regularization methods (Tibshirani, 1996); the regularization for support vector machines (Hastie et al., 2004); the Elastic Net, which is a mixture of the LASSO and Ridge Regression (Zou and Hastie, 2005); or a regularization scheme for neural networks, aimed at improving the classification margin (Ludwig et al., 2014).

Finally, Bayesian Statistics constitute an alternative approach to frequentist statistics (as are the methods describe above) in both terms of decision theory and inference. Though their potential in the social sciences and economy was pointed out almost 40 years ago (Harsanyi, 1978), the complex numerical integrations needed made them remain unused. However, the recent advances in computation methods have made it possible to easily apply Bayesian methods (Congdon, 2007).

To mention some, Bayesian Model Averaging (BMA) is a multimodeling method that is starting to be applied to linear regression and generalized linear models (Ley and Steel, 2012). Naive Bayes, which is a machine learning tool for classification whose popularity is starting to increase due to its simplicity for being implemented, being fast and computationally efficient, and obtaining high classification accuracy, especially for Big Data (Wu et al., 2015). Also, the Spike-and-Slab Regression, which is a variable selection method for linear regression models (Varian, 2014). Besides of this, the Bayesian Structural Time Series (BSTS) technique is devoted to treating panel or longitudinal

data, which are very common in the social sciences. This is a method for
variable selection and time series forecasting and nowcasting, used as an
alternative to traditional time series analysis methods such as Autorregressive
(AR) or Moving Average (MA) models.

2.4.3 Methods for assessing models' performance and robustness

A basic objective in any data analysis focused on forecasting is to obtain a
robust model with the best out-of-sample predictive precision possible. In
this section, a brief review on techniques for improving the performance of
forecasting and nowcasting models is provided.

Assessing the performance and robustness of predictive models is essential
to determine their validity and applicability, and the quality of the predictions.
In this case, performance refers to how well a model fits the data and how accurate it is, while robustness refers to how well a model works on alternate
data, that is, on data which is different from that used to build the model. If
a model has a good performance, then it is capable of detecting the characteristics in a data set and providing highly accurate predictions. Moreover, if it
is robust, then the predictions obtained could generalize and so the model is
valid and useful with new data. The goal in any big data analysis is to build
models that are the same time robust and provide accurate outputs: this is the
only path to use them as reliable tools for forecasting and nowcasting whose
results can be used for decision-making.

To compare and select different kind of models depending on how well
they fit to data and how complex they are, there exist uncountable classically applied tests such as Nagelkerke's R^2, Hosmer-Lemeshow, Mallows' Cp,
Akaike Information Criterion (AIC), Bayesian Information Criterion (BIC),
Deviance or Log-Likelihood, among others. Although these tests and indices
provide useful information about model performance, they were not conceived
for treating the huge amount of complex data with which we work nowadays.
The particular characteristics and issues of big data (size, bias, imbalanced

sets, complex relations...) make necessary to complement classical tests with more recently developed techniques that are capable to better deal with these issues (Varian, 2014).

First of all, to ensure that the predictions obtained are robust it is recommended to build the models by conducting a holdout process in which the initial sample is split into two subsets: the training set and the test set. The former is used to train the model, and generally includes about 75% to 90% of the initial observations, while the latter is used to evaluate its predictive performance and includes the remaining percentage of observations. Even if data is large enough, it may be divided in three sets: a train set (the largest), a validation set and a test set. This method ensures that the predictions obtained are robust, so that they can be generalized to an independent data set. Another approach with the same objective is K-Fold Cross-Validation. In this method, data is split into K parts of equal size and the model is fitted K times, where K-1 parts are used to train the model and the remaining is used to test its predictive performance. Finally, the K estimates of the prediction error are combined. In case each part includes just one observation, then the process is called Leave-one-out Cross Validation (Hastie et al., 2013). For big data sets, the first method is recommended.

In addition, for properly training classifiers, at least the train set should be balanced, because this way the model is built to successfully detect each of the categories equally. Otherwise the learning process could be endangered (Menardi and Torelli, 2014). A sample is balanced when each of the categories of the response variable is present in the same proportion. To balance an unbalanced data set, solutions such as oversampling, undersampling, synthetic sampling or kernel methods can be applied (He and Garcia, 2009). Unbalanced data sets are common in social sciences, so it is expected that the use of these procedures in socio-economic research will expand in the near future.

Moreover, think if what we are trying to predict is if someone is infected with a disease; then, the best situation would be to obtain a true negative (individual not infected). That is, not only false positives, but also false negatives, imply costs. It is important to assign a monetary value to these costs in order to influence the decision making of a model. This process is known as "Cost-sensitive analysis" (Sun et al., 2007). It makes use of the Cost Matrix, which reflects the costs and benefits associated to each of the four possible outcomes of a classifier. Providing this information to a classifier, it can be influenced to minimize the most costly errors or to maximize beneficial classifications, so that we obtain a "weighted accuracy". Similarly, by using Loss Functions, classifiers are forced to give preference to predictors that help to predict true probabilities accurately (Witten et al., 2016).

To check the predictive accuracy of classifiers, methods such as the Lift analysis, Precision-Recall Curves, ROC Curves and the Confusion Matrix are pertinent, whose fundamentals and applications regarding the social sciences can be looked at (Fawcett, 2006) and (Witten et al., 2016). When the output variable is not categorical, but numerical, other measures are available, such as the Root Mean Squared Error (RMSE), the Percentage Error (PE), the Fractional Bias or the Index of Agreement (IA), whose popularity is starting to increase.

2.5 The data lifecycle

Digital data have many advantages, such as being easy to share, replicate and recombine, which make them potentially reusable. Business and researchers can take advantage of this to boost research in progress and leverage past investments, for instance. However, to exploit all the benefits of digital data, they must be properly collected, processed and preserved. Data loss or damage may imply economic costs as well as lost chances, reason why funder agents (public or private) are increasingly demanding institutions to document and run data-management plans taking into account the whole lifecycle of data (Lynch, 2008). For this reason, it is basic to define what phases and processes form this lifecycle in order to implement robust and flexible architectures to manage data in the context of the Digital Era.

The data lifecycle is the sequence of stages that data follow from the moment they enter a system to the moment they are erased from the system or stored (Simonet et al., 2015). Between the data entrance and exit or storage, data go through different stages, which may differ depending on the type of data and purpose to achieve as documented in the compilation of classic data lifecycles (Committee on Earth Observation Satellites - Working Group on Information Systems and Services, 2012). The Knowledge Discovery in Databases (KDD) process was the first proposal of a model to manage digital data (Fayyad et al., 1996). It refers to the complete (non-cyclical) process of extracting knowledge from data, and includes five main stages: data selection, data pre-processing, data transformation, data mining and data interpretation. As databases started to exponentially grow in size and complexity, the necessity of a wider scheme to appropriately manage these data was highlighted, especially by the industry. This derived into the development of the Cross-Industry Standard Process for Data Mining (CRISP-DM process), which is an expanded implementation of the KDD process that introduced the management of digital data as a cycle (Chapman et al., 2000). It comprises six stages: business understanding, data understanding, data preparation, modelling, evaluation and deployment. If both are compared, the first and last stages of CRISP-DM process are new with respect to the KDD process, while the "data understanding" stage of CRISP-DM is similar to the "data pre-processing" and "data transformation" stages of KKD.

The next approach to data management within a digital environment that the scientific and industrial community focused on, and to which most research efforts have been paid since these days, was called itself the "data lifecycle". The Data Documentation Initiative Alliance (DDI Alliance) was one of the first voices to focus their efforts on this idea (DDI Alliance, 2008). It proposed a data lifecycle including the following five stages: first, discovery and planning; second, initial data collection; third, final data preparation and analysis; fourth, publication and sharing; and last, long-term management. This departing point considers from planning the project (what is being studied, what data are needed and how they are going to be treated, etc.) to determining how to store and preserve data in the long-term. With respect to KDD and

CRISP-DM processes, this is a more extensive approach that includes basic concepts within digital data such as sharing and long-term management.

Afterwards, Corti et al. (2014) described the phases and activities typically undertaken within the research data lifecycle. These phases, each of which included a number of specific activities, are the following: discovery and planning, data collection, data processing and analysis, publishing and sharing, long-term management and reusing data. This proposal extends the initial one by DDI Alliance to include an additional stage at the end of the cycle devoted to data reuse. A more exhaustive data lifecycle to date was proposed by Rüegg et al. (2014), who included up to eight stages: the first four stages (planning, data collection, data quality control, and analysis) correspond to managing data in a traditional project which is new (no previously results or data exist). If the project relies on existing data (referred to as "data reuse"), then it follows the third first stages and continues with additional data discovery, data integration, and finally, the analysis.

While Corti et al. (2014) considers data reuse as a step itself, Rüegg et al. (2014) reference data reuse as a type of project in which existing data are used, including some steps within this lifecycle. The context of economic and social analysis makes it more appropriate to consider data reuse as a step itself, given that as a project that started from scratch develops and data are obtained and exploited, these data may be reused many times in the same project with different purposes. That is, the view that a project is new or departs from data seems excessively static for economic and social nowcasting purposes. Additionally, to complete each of the data lifecycles, this work includes two more steps (presumably as final steps): data documentation and data archiving in a public repository, which we consider basic for preserving and publishing data.

The review of these works of reference allowed us to integrate and fully describe the different stages of a full data lifecycle in the context of economic and social analysis. Its aim is to standardize the concept of data lifecycle and serve as framework when it comes to designing a proper data management architecture in this context. Our proposal for a data lifecycle includes nine stages, as reflected in Figure 2.3. These stages are described as follows:

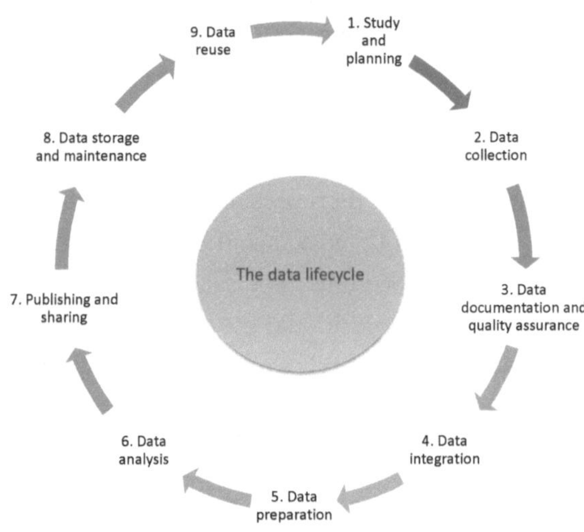

Figure 2.3: The data lifecycle within a Big Data paradigm

1. **Study and planning**: This first stage consists in designing the research or business project to achieve the desired goals of funders or managers. Once each phases of the study is defined, it is necessary to plan what procedures to treat data (collected or generated throughout the research) will be applied. For instance, this includes planning what type of data are going to be collected, how and from which sources, which methods will be used for their processing and analysis, where will they be stored, and to find out what legal regulations and privacy issues affect the type of data that is going to be analyzed, in order to adapt the operating procedures.

2. **Data collection**: This stage consists in accessing the sources, which can
   be internal or external, and collect initial or raw data. Depending on
   the field of knowledge and the data required for developing the project,
   activities such as phenomena observation, experimentation, recording,
   simulating, scraping or negotiating with third-party data providers will
   be part of this stage.

3. **Data documentation and quality assurance**: This stage consists
   in documenting the acquired data and checking their quality. First,
   the data acquisition process should be documented by associating data
   to metadata. The metadata include information related to the source of
   origin, data format, technical details on the retrieval process or accessing
   dates, among others, thus enabling their reuse and correct referencing.
   Second, data quality and validity should be assured. It is required to
   verify the trustworthiness of the data sources as well as of the own data,
   to control for any data inconsistencies, such as unexpected values or
   typing errors, and to clean and anonymize data if necessary.

4. **Data integration**: This stage consists in fusing data obtained from different data sources with a coherent and homogeneous structure, which
   helps to make data traceable and easier to access and manipulate in suc-
   cessive projects. This can include activities such as establishing relations
   among variables of different data sources, adapting units, translating, or
   creating a single database with all the acquired data. Data integration
   should also incorporate privacy constraints to avoid disclosing some private information in the integrated data. This is a major concern because
   rich integrated data may facilitate discovering some personal details otherwise anonymous.

5. **Data preparation**: This stage consists in transforming data so that
   they meet the format requirements of the analysis tools and techniques
   that are going to be applied. This includes activities such as transcribing,

digitizing, interpolating, establish a tabular format in the data set or deriving new data by operating with the existing data.

6. **Data analysis**: This stage consists in analyzing data, obtaining and interpreting results, and achieving conclusions. A huge range of statistical techniques and computational tools are called to be used in this stage. The final selection of the most appropriate techniques will depend on the type of data analyzed and research objectives. The interpretation of the results and conclusions achieved, as well as the results themselves, are basic inputs for the next stage.

7. **Publishing and sharing**: This stage consists in publishing results and conclusions derived from data analysis, or the generated data sets themselves. The outputs of this stage aim to facilitate the decision-making process of managers or policy-makers (when data is presented in reports, for instance), to spread knowledge (if a research article is published, for instance) and to feed automatic systems of companies with information of relevance to help the staff make decisions such as ordering supplies, among many others. Other related activities in this stage are establishing copyright of data and results, authoring publications, citing data sources, distributing data and controlling data access.

8. **Data storage and maintenance**: This stage consists in archiving and registering all the data gathered, processed and analyzed, for allowing long-term data preservation, curation and reuse. Actions to be done may include storing data in specific repositories or computational systems, migrating them to other platforms or mediums, regularly backing up the data, producing associated metadata, preserving the documentation generated during the whole process, controlling data security and privacy and erasing data if required by legal regulations, for instance.

9. **Data reuse**: This stage consists in reusing data that has been previously gathered, processed, analyzed and stored. This action can be originated in a variety of different purposes such as testing new hypotheses related

to the same project for which data were collected, sharing or selling data to companies, conducting new projects for which existing data can be useful or using data with instructive purposes.

2.6 A Big Data Architecture for nowcasting and forecasting social and economic changes

Our proposal of a Big Data architecture for nowcasting social and economic changes is presented in Figure 2.4. Departing from the approach of the data lifecycle in the organization, it includes layers and modules to manage the processing and integration of social and economic data, including the storage, processing policies and publication of results.

This architecture is organized in three layers. The data analysis layer contains the main processes of generating knowledge from the input data: from the ingestion of data from multiple sources to the publication of reports. Together with this layer, there are two other layers that work as support to the data analysis: The governance layer is in charge of applying policies and regulations to the whole data lifecycle, as well as managing the licences related to the data sets. The persistence layer deals with the storage and management of data to make them available to the different modules in the data analysis layer.

2.6.1 Data analysis layer

The data analysis layer is the part of the architecture that implements the main processes required to generate knowledge, in form of reports or predictions, from the different data sources to which the organization has access. It is composed of six modules that work sequentially, from the data reception to the publishing of results.

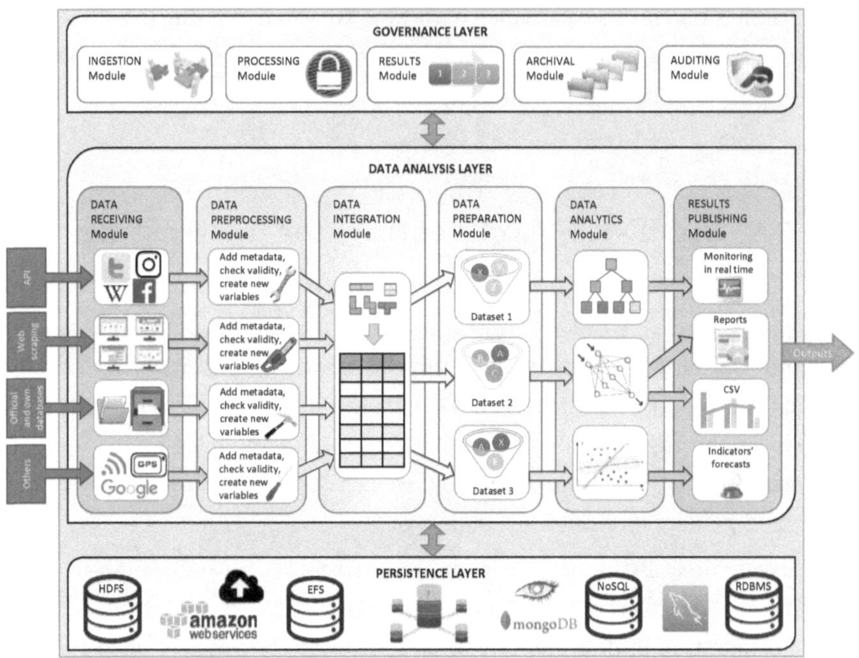

Figure 2.4: Big Data architecture for nowcasting and forecasting social and
economic changes

2.6.1.1 Data receiving module

This module constitutes the data ingestion point in the architecture, so that
data external to the system are made accessible to the other modules of the
architecture. This way, external data are connected to the processing stream
of the nowcasting system. It is composed of different elements, as many as
different data sources are used as input.

Connected data sources can be classified into two main groups: First,
those sources owned by the organization implementing the architecture. These
sources may include relational databases managing the daily operation of the
company, that is, business-specific information, such as sales, customers, pur-

chases, website analytics, and so on. Own sources also involve data not directly generated by the business operation, but collected or requested by the organization at variable frequencies. This includes surveys, market research data, and non-periodic report data.

The second group of data sources are those external, that is, those sources which are not controlled by the organization, though they may contain information relevant to its operation. A wide variety of sources may be considered as relevant for the organization purposes. For instance, some open data offered by public institutions might provide some information on the context of the company customers. Similarly, social and economic data published by the official statistics institutions have also potential for explaining the context in which individuals make decisions. Google Trends and social media platforms, such as Twitter or Facebook, are useful sources for detecting trends and relations between relevant topics. Furthermore, many other web sites or RSS providing product opinions, political comments, product releases, etc. might be explored to find some other contextual variables that could complement own data sources.

Since the access to these sources is wildly heterogeneous, the elements of this data receiving module must hide the complexity for accessing the sources. The access to these sources by the different elements in the module may be done by means of an Application Programming Interface (API) when available from the data provider, or by means of specific software developed for this purpose, e.g., web scraper.

All elements in this module will receive the data with the format and structure provided by the origin, which could be incompatible among them. According to their structure, data can be classified as structured, semi-structured or unstructured. Structured data includes information organized at high level, such as in relational databases, which apart from data, contains a schema with restrictions and relations. Semi-structured data also has some organization of the information, although the schema is embedded in the data. That is, its structure is self-describing, as in XML documents. Unstructured data provide no structure at all, and can be considered as a collection of elements. This does not mean that each element does not have a structure, but that the schema has not been described, so additional techniques to infer some structure should be applied. Text documents are typical unstructured sources. Data structure is a key factor to succeed integrating data from different sources, as it is the first step to establish the links between them. Structured data are usually related to SQL databases, while NoSQL are more suitable for storing unstructured and semi-structured data.

The elements in this module could access origins in batch or in stream. Stream processing is possible when the source allows access with high bandwidth and low latency conditions, e.g., when accessing an own relational database. However, when access conditions are not so favourable, the elements should work in batch, thus requiring persistent storage for the accessed data. In such event, the type of storage (SQL or NoSQL) must be consistent with the data source type. In any case, the data access that this module provides to the remaining modules of the architecture should be given as in stream processing.

2.6.1.2 Data preprocessing module

This module departs from the data connections prepared in the data receiving module. It aims to validate and preprocess data to leave them ready for integrating different sources. This preprocessing is divided in three steps.

The first step is to record and document the procedure of data acquisition by attaching metadata to the original source. These metadata should include information about the data source, the version of the collector (in the receiving module) used for the retrieval, the schema with the data structure (if any) and other technical details such as the codification, format and so on.

The second step is to check the internal validity of each source. Although structured sources usually keep all observations in the right format, other sources may be internally inconsistent. Thus, this step involves checking observations for anomalous values (e.g., text when a number is expected) and dealing with them, for instance, by marking them as missing or wrong. This

may result in a number of useless observations, that is, those with an excessive
number of missing features, which may be cleaned up to avoid including noise
in the data analysis process.

The third step is related to the extraction of features and the generation
of new data derived from the original source. At this step, only derived data
at entity level should be created. That is, if the origin provides rows, only
data from each row may be used to generate new features. If the origin
provides documents, only document contents may be used to generate variables
describing the document, for instance, by applying natural language processing
techniques. Examples of entity-level derived data may include counting the
number of words of a comment, detecting the language or computing the
term frequency. Derived data whose computation requires analyzing several
entities (e.g., computing an average) should be generated in the data analytics
module. When the computational effort to generate new data is high, the
resulting features should be persisted to allow for reusing them in subsequent
data integrations. This involves using a database consistent with the structure
type of the origin.

2.6.1.3 Data integration module

The objective of this module is to merge the different data sources and provide
homogeneous access to all data available to the organization. To do so, data
integration must deal with five challenges: i) heterogeneous sources, whose access was homogenized by the data receiving module; ii) related data structures
whose relation has not been explicitly established by the sources; iii) a variety
of data sizes and probably inconsistent formats; iv) heterogeneous time frequencies, ranging from milliseconds to years; and v) heterogeneous geographic
groupings, ranging from detailed GPS coordinates to state or country level.

To relate data from different sources, it is required to define schemes that
establish the relation among them. For instance, establishing the relation of
a commercial establishment to a region, it will be possible to relate its sales
to the average income of the area in which it is located. These data usually

come from different sources: sales are accessed through internal sources, while the average income could be provided by an official statistics institute.

To establish such relations, some linkage techniques and hierarchical groupings might be applied. Geographic hierarchies are useful to link records to the most appropriate geographic level, which is not necessarily the lowest one. For instance, street-level economic situation may be useful for analyzing housing prices, but it is too specific for a business whose influence area is wider, e.g., an airline office. Linkage techniques are required when the same entity does not receive the same identifier across the different sources. This could happen simply because it is written in a different language (e.g., the country name), situation which can be solved with a simple translation; but also because of lacking of a standardized or public id. In such cases, some analysis to match the record could help find relations and provide new insights on the data.

Adapting time frequencies is also included in this category. It is required to adopt some criteria to generate high frequency data from lower frequencies and vice versa. Reducing time frequencies may involve computing some summarizing statistics (e.g., average, maximum, etc), while increasing time frequencies may involve interpolating data or selecting the closest value in time.

Once several data sources are integrated and their relations are established, they could be stored in the persistence layer and feed the data analysis layer again as a new element in the data receiving module. This way, it is possible to use these sources as a single one when integrating with additional sources.

2.6.1.4 Data preparation module

The organization in which data are stored after the integration may not be suitable to perform the analysis. This module takes the data as prepared by the data integration module and transforms them to match the format expected by the data analytics module. Since each element in the analytics module may expect data in a different format, data preparation is also specific to each analytics element.

These transformations may involve grouping some elements or joining data from different tables to enrich the information about each entity or individual. This is also the most suitable module to alleviate the missing data, which may be estimated or interpolated to avoid losing cases.

A common operation in this module is the pivot transformation. Storing information as key-value pairs, in which entity features are spread among many rows, is quite convenient in Big Data environments. However, this may not be the table format expected by the analysis software. By applying the pivot transformation, all features regarding the same entity are arranged in the same row, which is the data organization commonly required to feed the analysis.

The resulting data after the preparation process should be stored to provide consistent input to the analysis. After conducting data integration and depending on the purpose of each particular study, it is possible to obtain small data sets derived from the initial big data set, which could be treated with traditional statistical techniques. The storage in this module must be analysis-driven, unlike the previous modules, whose storage is source-driven.

2.6.1.5 Data analytics module

This module applies statistical and machine learning methods to extract knowledge and make predictions from the data prepared by the previous module. To do so, descriptive and predictive techniques are applied. The descriptive analysis could provide some insights on the characteristics and evolution of the socio-economic variables under study. Its results will be used in the Results Publishing module to create tables and graphics representing the relationship among variables.

Predictive techniques are based on models that help explain, classify, forecast or nowcast the socio-economic variables under study. To do so, the models are estimated or trained by using learning methods and relying on any of the methods described in Section 2.4 for selecting the most meaningful variables and improving predictions. The computing-intensive nature of these techniques makes it difficult to deal with large data sets, since they do not properly scale when data size grows.

Before using the models, they must be validated with a different set of data than that used for estimation or training. The validation provides an estimation on the robustness of the models and the quality of the predictions, so that the risk related to an inaccurate prediction can be taken into account.

The methods used in this module may be applied in stream (i.e., the models are continuously being trained with new data), scheduled (i.e., the models are trained periodically), or on demand (i.e, the user manually requests to train again the models). Choosing one or other approach depends mainly on the computational resources available for this module.

The main output of the predictive techniques are the trained models, whose application can guide the operative and the strategy of the organization. They are made available to the rest of the organization by means of the results publishing module.

2.6.1.6   Results publishing module

The purpose of this module is to provide the organization with a decision-making tool. To do so, it makes the results of the analysis conducted in the data analytics module available to the organization, which includes the people that make decisions, but also other information systems that could benefit from the data analysis. For this reason, this module should offer the results in different formats, adapted to the different consumers of information in the organization.

The publication of results for decision-makers should be done in the form of reports, including tables, graphics and other visual elements that help understand the social and economic behavior behind the data. The main objective of these reports is to support decisions at strategic or tactical levels.

Making the analysis results available to other information systems in the organization contributes to support the decision-making at operational level. There is a wide variety of options to do so. For instance, a trained model can be stored in a database or in any other storage for being applied by different business units. The model could also be offered as a service (under the SaaS paradigm) so that when a new event occurs, the service offers the prediction as a result of applying the model. This way, the trained models can be successfully applied to some operational actions such as purchases and financial resources management.

2.6.2 Governance layer

This layer is horizontal to the rest of the system and applies the organization policies and regulations to the whole data lifecycle: from the data ingestion to the disposal. It is composed of five modules, four of them related to the data lifecycle, plus one for auditing purposes:

- **Ingestion module**: It deals with the management of the sources, including the licenses and allowed uses, credentials for accessing them, internal user permissions, completeness of metadata, and so on.

- **Processing module**: It manages the privacy and anonymization policies, controls processing for ethical principles, keeps track of the transformations, as well as of the permissions for accessing the data and computing resources.

- **Results module**: It is concerned with the traceability of the results (from the sources to the final report), the permissions for accessing the reports and results, along with the privacy aspects that may affect the reports.

- **Archival and disposal module**: It implements the policy for archiving and disposing the information related to data sources, processing procedures and generated reports.

- **Auditing module**: It inspects that the implementation is consistent with the current regulations, as well as with the security and privacy policies. It may also include checking the overall performance of the architecture in order to ensure that the system has an acceptable response time.

2.6.3 Persistence layer

The persistence layer supports the other layers by managing all issues related to the storage needs. Its main function is associated with the storage of the data used as input in the data analysis layer, including the schema for describing the relations among sources and other meta-data. Not only the data itself is covered, but also the storage of the procedures followed in the different modules to access and transform the data.

Furthermore, this layer serves the data analytics and results publishing modules by providing storage for the results. This includes storing the models and providing them with the inputs required for computing new predictions or estimations as part of the publication of the results.

It is in the persistence layer where the storage infrastructure is controlled and managed. This layer will typically use distributed storage systems, combining local storage with cloud solutions that allow elastic storage and large volume data. The decision on whether to use local or cloud storage mainly depends on where (on- or off-premises) the modules intensive in computing power (e.g., data analytics) are implemented.

2.7 Conclusions

In the Digital Era, most economic and social behaviors leave behind a huge digital footprint, which is incipiently being used with nowcasting and forecasting purposes. Despite the enormous potential of these data, integrating and analyzing the wide variety of heterogeneous sources cannot be tackled with the traditional methods used in economics and social sciences. To succeed in this purpose, it is mandatory to carefully plan and implement the whole process of data extraction, transformation and analysis. This is the point in which the

Big Data and data lifecycle paradigms arise as helpful perspectives on how to
deal with this process.

This paper has proposed a novel Big Data architecture that accounts for
the particularities of the economic and social behavior analysis in the Digital
Era. The first particularity is related to the variety of sources that could
provide information about economic and social topics. Our first contribution
addresses this issue by reviewing the multiple data sources and proposing a
taxonomy to classify them according to the purpose of the agent generating
the data.

Following the Big Data paradigm, this wide variety of heterogeneous
sources requires specific methods for processing them. The second contribution of the paper addresses this issue by reviewing those methods not so
commonly used in the social sciences, and classifying them according to the
phase of the data analysis they operate.

In order to frame the data analysis in an organizational perspective and
allow its management in a robust and flexible architecture, the data lifecycle
approach has been taken. Different perspectives on this approach have been
reviewed and synthesized to establish and define all the involved phases and
processes.

Finally, the main contribution of the paper is the proposal of a Big Data
architecture adapted to the particularities of the economic and social analysis,
and grounded on the data lifecycle approach for the management of data
in the organization. At the same time, the proposal aimed to be general
enough to be implemented with different technologies, computing paradigms
and analytical software depending on the requirements and purposes of each
particular case. By implementing this architecture, an organization will be
able to make the most of all social and economic sources of information to
which it has access. Not only the organization of sources is advantageous, but
also their integration and connection to Big Data analytics tools able to run
the models for nowcasting and forecasting socio-economic variables. The wide
variety of data sources and techniques considered in the architecture results
in potentially more accurate and granular predictions.

Governments and official statistics institutions may also benefit from the implementation of an information system with the proposed architecture. Integrating the multiple sources to which they have access may result in improved predictions about key economic indicators and planning economic policies accordingly.

Although the proposed architecture is general enough to be implemented with any technology, its adoption is not without obstacles. To mention some of them, the integration of the architecture in the existing organizational information systems is a critical process to ensure the smooth generation of forecasts and nowcasts. The implementation of the modules in a proper cloud computing environment so that the system can scale easily is also crucial. As future work, we plan to implement the proposed Big Data architecture, in order to generate and publish some real-time nowcasts and forecasts of some socio-economic variables using Internet data.

Chapter 3

Web data mining for monitoring business export orientation

Chapter 3 is an adapted version of this published research paper:

- Title: Web data mining for monitoring business export orientation
- Authors: Desamparados Blazquez and Josep Domenech
- Year of publication: 2018
- Journal: Technological and Economic Development of Economy
- Volume: 24(2)
- Pages: 406-428
- DOI: 10.3846/20294913.2016.1213193

3.1   Introduction

New information is being published daily on the WWW, which has become
the largest public source of real-time information in the world. This increased
amount of online information is known as "Big Data", which are transforming
the economy and society. This data revolution is called to change, in the near
future, the landscape of economic policy and research (Einav and Levin, 2014;
Varian, 2014) as it is the main driver of the process of social change in the
ICTs era. As the scope of web technology in society grows, the data stream
increases, which makes people even thirstier for information. This kind of loop
process ends up with lots more information posted and updated on the net
(Edelman, 2012; Einav and Levin, 2014). In fact, the WWW has changed the

way people and companies interact and communicate. For these reasons, web technology doubtlessly opens up the possibility of improving economic and social policy and research, and has the potential to become the reference for real-time information.

The digital nature of the WWW makes it easy for computer programs to explore and analyze its contents, which enables automatic knowledge discovery and lowers the cost of the information retrieval process (Edelman, 2012). Such automatic information extraction opens up the possibility to build up-to-date indicators, which can be useful for a wide range of purposes. This is especially interesting for computing real-time economic indicators without waiting for official data, which are usually released after a long delay. In the particular context of the increasing economic globalization, a topic of much interest about the economy is the engagement in international commerce.

Establishing in foreign markets contributes to the long-term development of firms and economies (Miskinis and Reinbold, 2010; Zeng et al., 2012). Within the existing alternatives to establish in foreign markets, export is considered the easiest and fastest one. In addition, it represents an attractive and manageable opportunity for firms independently of their size (Nassimbeni, 2001; Majocchi et al., 2005). Export-oriented companies contribute to increase the competitiveness of an economy, since they become more proactive and adaptable to turbulent environments. For these reasons, exports figure prominently in the minds of policymakers (Girma et al., 2004).

To properly design and control export promotion policies, an accurate monitoring system should be implemented. However, current monitoring systems entail some concerns, such as the cost of producing the indicators, over-aggregation of data and the lag between implementing a specific policy and its effect on overseas sales (Wholey and Hatry, 1992; Spence, 2003). Policy monitoring can be enriched by obtaining firm-level data in real time, which would turn it into a continuous process with a higher level of granularity. This would allow to immediately collect changes in the microeconomic situation to improve their identification and understanding for researchers and policymakers.

In addition to the chance offered by technology to apply Big Data analysis on realtime data, the WWW has the ability to remove a number of geographic constraints and to facilitate instant communication worldwide, thus empowering exports (Dholakia and Kshetri, 2004; Vivekanandan and Rajendran, 2006). Therefore, corporate websites could reflect the export orientation of firms in different ways, a reflection which would gradually grow as Internet penetration deepens. Confirming this tendency, a previous work demonstrated that adoption of web technology and some web features are good predictors of firms' export orientation (Blazquez and Domenech, 2014). Unfortunately, this proposal to obtain an indicator of export orientation with web-based variables relies on a manual retrieval, which renders them inappropriate for designing a real-time monitoring system.

Given the importance of exports to the evolution of an economy, the availability of a new source of prompt information about firm export orientation becomes especially useful. This paper focuses on developing a new monitoring method which relies on automatically obtaining an indicator for the export orientation of firms by analyzing their corporate websites. This way, we can design a model for nowcasting not only the export orientation of a firm, but also of an economic sector or of a region. Nowcasting models exploit the early availability of variables correlated with the target one to obtain an "early estimate" before the official figure becomes available (Choi and Varian, 2009b; Banbura et al., 2013). These real-time estimates can help policymakers to make informed decisions earlier.

To evaluate our proposal, we build a regression model in a first step with manual web-based variables and compare its predictive performance to a baseline model with firm economic variables. In a second step, after validating the web variables, we check the usefulness of their automatic version by comparing the predictive performance of the manual model to that of an automatic one. Hence this paper has two objectives: to examine the ability of some web-based variables to infer firms' export orientation; and to validate their automatic retrieval so that a nowcast model, which constitutes a real-time monitoring system, can be implemented.

The remainder of the paper is organized as follows. Section 3.2 reviews some related research on the automatic extraction of web features and now-casting, linking web activities to the economy and on the website features that are expected to be related to firms' export orientation. Section 3.3 describes the data used to carry out the performance analysis and shows the results for the baseline model and the manual web-based model. Section 3.4 explains the construction and validation of the automatic variables, and analyzes the prediction performance of the proposed automatic model. The last section draws some concluding remarks and provides directions for future work.

3.2 Theoretical background

This section provides background on linking web activities to firms' characteristics and on the automatic extraction of web features. First, we review the related literature; second, we focus on some website features that could provide valuable information on the export orientation of firms; finally, we review some firms' economic characteristics which have been usually related to export behavior.

3.2.1 Web data mining for science and economic indicators

The digital nature of the WWW makes it easy for computer programs to explore and analyze its contents, thus enabling Big Data techniques and automatic knowledge discovery. In this context, the automatic extraction of web indicators for economic purposes is an incipient research topic, although similar methods have been formerly applied to other purposes such as obtaining indicators for scientific production.

The first approach to systematically use the web as a source of information is the webometrics. These indicators rely on analyzing web page links to compute similar measures to some widespread bibliometrics indicators. The first related work attempted to equate hypertext links with publication cites to generate similar indicators to impact factors (Ingwersen, 1998; Smith, 1999).

The main drawback of this approach is that the large heterogeneity found
in the web hinders the reliability of such indicators (Smith, 1999; Vaughan
and Hysen, 2002). However, this heterogeneity was not a limitation when
the scientific production of universities or nations was analyzed (Wilkinson
et al., 2003; Scharnhorst and Wouters, 2006; Heimeriks et al., 2008). More
recent research has successfully focused on economic topics, such as obtaining
indicators for the financial situation of banks (Vaughan and Romero-Frias,
2010).

Another noteworthy approach to obtain economic indicators from web data
is using reports generated by Google Trends (GT). This tool provides up-to-
date reports on the volume of web search queries with some specific text. These
data can be used to nowcast some economic variables because some specific
text querying (e.g., "apply for unemployment benefits") might correlate with
some particular aspect of economy (e.g., unemployment). Since they were first
introduced as an economic indicator by Choi and Varian (2009b), nowcasting
models with GT data have been applied to a number of situations, such as
proposing indicators for investors' attention (Da et al., 2011), tourist arrivals
(Bangwayo-Skeete and Skeete, 2015), business performance (Vaughan, 2014),
transaction volumes on the stock market (Preis et al., 2010; Moat et al., 2014),
and well-being (Askitas, Zimmermann 2015). Although GT can supply useful
hints on the economic activity at an aggregate level, its ability for characteriz-
ing individual firms is limited because it only provides data about what users
demand.

Individual firm strategies can be better observed on their corporate websites. In this context, Libaers et al. (2010) constructed a taxonomy of technology commercialization models by counting the appearance of some keywords
on firms' websites. This analysis was conducted by automating Google queries
with each potentially related keyword. The keyword analysis method for tracking firms' strategies has also been used by Youtie et al. (2012) and Arora et al.
(2013) in the emerging technologies context.

Beyond the keyword analysis, the first attempt to combine different website
features to perform a completely automatic analysis of corporate websites

to retrieve economic indicators was introduced by Domenech et al. (2012). This research work presented an architecture for a web data mining system that manages the download and analysis of corporate websites. The proposed system was applied to find web-based indicators for the size of companies. In this paper, we extend this system to deal with website features related to the export orientation of firms. Section 3.4 provides more details on the system implementation.

3.2.2 Export-related indicators built from website features

Web technologies and online platforms have made it possible for companies, independently of their size, to enter new markets and to increase their export sales thanks to the removal of geographical constraints and the instant communication all over the world. In fact, the WWW can at once remove some organizational and resource constraints which exporting presumably entails (Vivekanandan and Rajendran, 2006; Sinkovics et al., 2013).

At an aggregate level, a number of recent studies revealed that the Internet stimulates trade. For instance, it has been checked that expanding Internet use improves information availability, reduces trade-related costs (informational and transactional, among others) and boosts exports. Moreover, it has been found that an increase in the number of Internet users reduces asymmetric information, increases the business competition level and cuts fixed trade costs, thus contributing to export growth, as verified in the food and manufacturing industries (Clarke and Wallsten, 2006; Bojnec and Fertö, 2009, 2010).

Focusing on the WWW, the work by Freund and Weinhold (2004) revealed that growth in the number of websites in a country explains its export growth in the following year, since the Internet reduces market-specific fixed costs of trade. In addition, the WWW is useful for increasing firm's visibility and potential customers, and to also improve operational efficiency. This is due to its capacity to make communications and transactions easier and less expensive, which means important efficiency gains (Dholakia and Kshetri, 2004; Kazemikaitiene and Bileviciene, 2008; Berthon et al., 2012).

Corporate websites have been used in previous works to infer firms' economic characteristics. In line with this, Overbeeke and Snizek (2005) reviewed company websites to find indicators of corporate culture, while Meroño-Cerdan and Soto-Acosta (2007) related web content to firm performance. Similarly, Llopis et al. (2010) used corporate website contents to analyze firm strategies. Firm export orientation can also be found on website adoption, as described by Blazquez and Domenech (2014). Therefore at an individual firm's level, a number of website features could be linked to company international strategies.

For all these reasons, we review how different website features could provide valuable information on the export orientation of firms. The objective is to verify whether these features differ between the corporate websites of exporters and non exporters, thus enabling to build a web-based predictive model. To do so, we classified web features in two different groups according to their nature: the "Web presence" group and the "Content-based" group.

Web presence variables   The first group of variables is related to how and when firms implement a corporate website. It includes two variables, namely the domain name age and top-level domain code.

Experienced firms are usually more likely to export as they have had time to increase their knowledge and accumulate useful resources for internationalization (Majocchi et al., 2005; Fernández and Nieto, 2006). Firms with more experience on the Internet could follow this same pattern towards export.

The domain name is the main identifier of a company on the Internet. The date on which a domain name is registered suggests the approximate date when a company started to go online (Scaglione et al., 2009), despite the temporal gap between a domain name being registered and a website being implemented (Murphy et al., 2007). Hence, the domain name age is related to the firm's experience in the Internet. As older firms usually own older domains, having an older domain could be indicative of a greater propensity to export.

The top-level domain (TLD), as part of the firm's Internet name, is either an ISO country code (e.g., .es for Spain) or a generic code (e.g., .com). According to Murphy and Scharl (2007), using a country code or a generic one reflects local or global interests, respectively. In addition, it is an important decision in the company's e-branding strategy (Ibeh et al., 2005). Thus, its election could be related to the firm's strategic orientation.

Current exporters or companies which intend to start exporting in the near future would prefer to choose any generic domain code to establish its presence on the Internet, as they have a more international profile. Therefore, a generic top-level domain could be positively related to the firm's export orientation.

Content-based variables   This group of variables refers to the contents and functions available in corporate websites. It includes two variables, namely the foreign language version and presence of export-related keywords.

Offering websites in more than one language is usually related to greater marketing effectiveness (Lee and Morrison, 2010). Moreover, deploying multilingual websites helps firms to succeed in reaching their target markets and to better deal with clients and suppliers as the cultural language barrier disappears and users feel more confident. In fact offering a multilingual website helps firms gain a competitive advantage in the global market, and enables them to reach a larger number of potential customers (Samiee, 2008; Escobar-Rodríguez and Carvajal-Trujillo, 2013). Therefore, a website being available in more than one language could be related to the foreign target markets of companies.

Across all languages, English seems the most natural option for exporting firms in non English speaking countries as it is the most widely used language in international businesses.

The WWW is being used as a marketing media by firms. Through their websites, firms can provide information about the markets and countries where they operate and can describe their products and services without limitations. This way, they can easily reach more potential customers throughout the world (Dholakia and Kshetri, 2004; Vivekanandan and Rajendran, 2006; Berthon et al., 2012).

Motiwalla et al. (2005) suggest that websites allow companies to gain marketing efficiencies. One fact that this relies on is that website information origination costs are lower than for printed catalogues (Bennett, 1997). These characteristics make websites appealing for companies so that they can include as much information about themselves as they consider necessary. In this way, business strategies can emerge on the WWW and they can be monitored by the presence of key terms, as demonstrated by recent research (Youtie et al., 2012; Arora et al., 2016).

For these reasons, if a firm is selling abroad or intends to reach new markets, it is likely that information about these matters is provided in its corporate website. These activities can be tracked by detecting the presence of certain keywords on websites. Consequently, presence of trade-related keywords on a corporate website could be positively related to the firm's export orientation.

3.2.3   Structural variables related to export orientation

To assess the prediction performance of the web-based variables, a baseline predictive model was built using the firms' structural variables which have been traditionally related to their export propensity. These included the size, labor productivity and age of the firm.

Firm size Firm size has been usually related to firm enrollment and performance in international activities. Its effect can differ depending on the industry and other variables considered for prediction, as shown in the literature. On the one hand, some authors emphasize that firm size positively impacts export behavior, as stated by the stage theory of internationalization. Larger firms have more resources, so they are better equipped to deal with the internationalization challenge (Majocchi et al., 2005; Fernández and Nieto, 2006). On the other hand, a number of studies have revealed that firm size is not a restriction in export performance. In fact, it is argued that firm size influences the firm's decision to enter international markets only when it remains under some specific level (Bonaccorsi, 1992; Pla-Barber and Alegre, 2007).

Firm labor productivity   The literature shows that exporters are generally more productive than non exporters. It is argued that this could be due to two alternative effects: the "learning-by-exporting" effect and the "self-selection" effect. The first establishes that the higher productivity of exporters comes from the international experience and knowledge that they acquire from their presence in international markets. The latter states that the most productive firms decide to enroll in exporting activities because they are better positioned to succeed and to recover the sunk costs associated with entering foreign markets. As pointed out in the literature, both effects may co-exist (Bernard and Jensen, 1995; Girma et al., 2004; Andersson et al., 2008). Among others, a frequently employed measure for firm performance is labor productivity.

Firm age   The firm's age, which is taken as a proxy to its experience, has been usually considered in the literature as being related to export orientation. However, results between different studies diverge. Some authors have found a positive relationship between the firm's age and its export behavior in both propensity and intensity terms. This can be explained because they have had more time to increase their knowledge, resources and capabilities, which are useful business tools to face the internationalization challenge (Majocchi et al., 2005; Fernández and Nieto, 2006).

Other studies have concluded that the firm's age is not that related to export behavior or that it has a negative effect, which is in line with the "born-global" phenomenon. This maintains that there are firms which have expanded into foreign markets since they were set up and did not need much time or lots of resources because of the role of innovation and ICTs (Baldauf et al., 2000; Andersson et al., 2004). The differences between studies could be due to two co-existing effects: the greater solidity and experience of older firms, which imply better conditions for exporting and, at the same time, the

more receptive and flexible nature of younger firms, which can make it easy
to adapt to the current quick changes in trends and markets.

3.3 Using web-based variables to infer firm export orientation

3.3.1 The sample

The sample for this study included 350 manufacturing companies (NACE Rev.
2 codes 10- 33) with corporate website established at the Region of Valencia,
in east Spain. According to INE (2012), the rate of industrial companies with
website in this region is 75.9%, similar to the rest of Spain (75%). The sample was retrieved through a simple random sampling design from the SABI[1]
database. As the list of corporate websites provided by SABI was incomplete,
the missing website URLs were obtained by querying a search engine with
the company's name or its VAT number, given that Spanish regulations make
firms include this information in their websites. From each website, the following web-based variables were manually retrieved and coded at the end of
2012:

- **Domain name's age** (DOM_AGE_i): Continuous variable measured as
  the number of years since the corporate website domain name was registered. It was computed from the information available in the Internet
  whois service.

- **Top-level domain** (TLD_i): Dichotomous variable that takes value 1
  in case the TLD of the corporate website was generic.

- **English version** (EN_i): Dichotomous variable that takes value 1 if the
  corporate website had a functional English version available.

---

[1]SABI: Sistema de Análisis de Balances Ibéricos. It is published by Bureau van Dijck. It
includes information about 5,000 active manufacturing firms with website in the Region of
Valencia.

- **Export-related keywords** ($KEYWORDS_i$): Dichotomous variable with value 1 if the website contained any term associated to exportation. A word list[2] containing key terms potentially connected to export orientation was prepared and searched for by querying Google with each term at each website using the advanced search tool.

In order to validate our proposal, this set of web-based variables was supplemented with some economic characteristics of the firms. This information was collected from the companies' financial statements, available in SABI, and the records of exporters of the Spanish Institute for Foreign Trade (ICEX) and the Spanish High Council of Chambers of Commerce. After downloading the websites, we had to wait more than one year to access to the economic information from year 2012, as it is made available with delay. Once our proposal is validated, we will be able to provide frequent estimations about firm export orientation without relying on official sources of data. The following variables were included:

- **Size of the firm** ($SIZE_i$): Continuous variable measured by the logarithm of the number of employees in the firm.

- **Firm's labor productivity** (LP_i): Continuous variable measured as the value added per employee.

- **Age of the firm** (AGE_i): Continuous variable measured as the number of years since the firm was established.

- **Firm's industry** ($INDUSTRY_i$): Vector of binary variables for two-digit NACE Rev. 2 codes used to control for specific industry effects. It included 14 variables, of which 13 corresponded to different industry categories with at least 10 companies in the sample. The remaining one gathered all those firms in sectors with fewer than 10 companies in the

---

[2]The terms included in the word list (mostly Spanish) were: Continental; continente; continentes; export; exporta; exportación; exportaciones; exportamos; exportando; exporter; extranjero; globalización; internacional; internacionales; internacionalización; mundial; países. These keywords were selected from our experience after visiting many corporate websites.

sample. Ensuring that each variable controls for 10 or more companies allows us to avoid overfitting.

- **Export orientation** ($EXPORT_i$): Dichotomous variable that takes value 1 if the firm was enrolled in exporting activities. It is the dependent variable in the prediction models.

3.3.2   Data analysis

First, some descriptive statistics were obtained, as Table 3.1 [3] shows. Firms with export activities accounted for 48.29% of the sample. It can be observed that the majority of the companies owned a generic domain. It is also remarkable that the mean firm age (20.24 years) was much larger than the mean domain name age (8.60 years). This means that firms have little experience in the Internet and that its adoption is a relatively recent practice, which predictably will continue to expand. In addition, the absence of high correlations (>0.7) among the variables means that there was no high risk of information redundancy and multicollinearity when estimating the prediction models.

Table 3.1: Descriptive statistics and correlation matrix

Variable	Mean	SD	1	2	3	4	5	6	7
1.$EXPORT_i$	0.48	0.50							
2.DOM_AGE_i	8.60	4.15	0.35***						
3.TLD_i	0.73	0.44	0.01	0.12**					
4.EN_i	0.39	0.49	0.56***	0.42***	0.06				
5.$KEYWORDS_i$	0.37	0.48	0.38***	0.29***	-0.01	0.33***			
6.$SIZE_i$	20.47	48.15	0.44***	0.40***	-0.15***	0.34***	0.29***		
7.LP_i	35.42	24.67	0.22***	0.18***	-0.10	0.15***	0.09***	0.20***	
8.AGE_i	20.24	10.82	0.33***	0.29***	-0.06	0.19***	0.19***	0.28***	0.17***

Notes: ***(p<0.01); **(p<0.05). The mean for variable $SIZE_i$ is expressed in levels instead of logarithms, as this is more informative on the behavior of the variable. However, all analyses were performed using the variable in logarithms

---

[3]Procedures employed: Pearson's r coefficient for pairs of continuous variables; Point-biserial coefficient for pairs of a continuous and a binary variable; and Phi coefficient for pairs of binary variables (Cohen et al., 2002).

Table 3.2 reflects the sector distribution of the firms in the sample. The metal products, textiles and furniture industries, which are highly representative of the Valencian manufacturing sector (Molina-Morales et al., 2011), predominate the sample.

Table 3.2: Sector distribution of the firms in the sample

NACE Rev. 2 Codes	N	%
10. Food products	26	7.43
13. Textiles	29	8.29
15. Leather and related products	18	5.14
16. Wood and products of wood and cork, except furniture; articles of straw and plaiting materials	18	5.14
18. Printing and reproduction of recorder media	26	7.43
20. Chemicals and chemical products	21	6.00
22. Rubber and plastic products	27	7.71
25. Fabricated metal products, except machinery and equipment	52	14.86
27. Electrical equipment	12	3.43
28. Machinery and equipment n.e.c	24	6.86
31. Furniture	28	8.00
32. Other manufacturing (jewelry, games and toys,etc)	13	3.71
33. Repair and installation of machinery and equipment	11	3.14
Various	45	12.86
Total	350	100

Notes: "Various" includes the firms under those NACE manufacturing codes with less than 10 firms.

In order to test whether the variables behaved differently depending on the firm's export orientation, statistical techniques of group differences were employed. Normality and homogeneity of variance were checked both graphically and numerically for the continuous variables. As none of the variables fulfilled both assumptions, the non-parametric Mann-Whitney U test was employed. For the case of the binary variables, the Pearson's Chi-squared test was employed (Anderson et al., 2014). The results of these analyses are reported in Table 3.3.

Within the domain name age, exporters owned significantly older domains than non exporters on average (10.1 years vs. 7.2 years). This suggests that

Table 3.3: Results of the comparison between exporters and non-exporters

Variable	Mean $EXPORT_i=1$	Mean $EXPORT_i=0$	Mann-Whitney U (Sig.)	Chi-squared (Sig.)
DOM_AGE_i	10.096	7.200	0.000	–
TLD_i	0.740	0.729	–	0.922
EN_i	0.675	0.127	–	0.000
$KEYWORDS_i$	0.562	0.193	–	0.000
$SIZE_i$	2.877	2.003	0.000	–
LP_i	40.912	30.200	0.000	–
AGE_i	23.924	16.807	0.000	–

a relationship between Internet experience and export behavior exists as exporters started the implementation of corporate websites earlier than non exporters. Furthermore, older firms have the possibility of owning older domains, thus the firm's experience, domain name age and enrollment in exporting activities are connected.

For TLD, no statistically significant differences between exporters and non exporters were found. This finding, though contrary to what was expected, is actually reasonable.

First, although a generic domain is related to e-business, it does not necessarily imply an international profile. Second, the legal and bureaucratic obstacles when registering Spanish domains, which were in force until 2005, probably made them less appealing than generic domains. This could have favored adopting the latter among the majority of firms.

Regarding an English website version, its availability was statistically higher for exporters (67.5%) than for non exporters (12.7%), which indicates that the relation between exports and the most widely used language in international trade is reflected on corporate websites. Presence of keywords on exporters' websites was higher than on the non exporters' ones (56.2% vs. 19.3%), and the difference was statistically significant. However, the positive percentage for non exporters websites suggests that some words considered in the analysis may not be appropriate for distinguishing between both groups of firms. An analysis on the separate effect of each export-related keyword was conducted when evaluating the automatic extraction of web features (see Section 3.4).

For the firm's structural variables, exporters showed higher values for the three variables under study (size, labor productivity and age of firm), and the differences were statistically significant in all cases. Therefore, they can be safely included in a baseline model to check the effectiveness of the web-based predictions.

Overall, the univariate analysis exhibited that exporters have earlier implemented corporate websites on which the availability of an English version and the presence of export-related keywords are also more frequent than for the websites of non exporters. These results bring up the potential of the information extracted from corporate websites for monitoring firms' export behavior. Regarding the structural variables, exporters seem larger, more experienced and more productive than non exporters.

3.3.3 The predictive models

This section describes the predictive model based on the variables retrieved from corporate websites, and compares its prediction performance against the baseline model based on firms' structural variables. To do this, two logistic regression models were built after identifying which characteristics varied across exporters and non exporters. The estimations of both models were compared to determine the validity of our proposal.

About the statistical methods, logistic regression was applied because it is the most appropriate when a dependent variable is binary, as is the case in this study. The selected variables were those that varied with an admissible level of significance ($p < 0.05$) between both groups of firms and did not correlate highly (Nassimbeni, 2001). According to these criteria, the web-based model was defined as follows:

$$Prob(EXPORT_i = 1) = \frac{e^{Z_i}}{1 + e^{Z_i}}; \quad (3.1)$$

$$Z_i = \beta_0 + \beta_1 DOM\_AGE_i + \beta_2 EN_i + \beta_3 KEYWORDS_i + \gamma INDUSTRY_i,$$

where β_0 is a constant and the coefficients β_1, β_2, β_3 and γ indicate the relative influence of each feature on the prediction of the category of the dependent variable. Table 3.4 shows the estimation results, including the estimated regression coefficients and the Standard Error (SE), p-value and Odds Ratio for these estimations. The Odds Ratio (OR) is a measure of association between the presence of a particular characteristic and the presence of exports, that is, our dependent variable. Thus, an OR greater than 1 indicates that the probability of being an exporter increases with a given independent variable, an OR lower than 1 indicates that this probability decreases, while OR equals 1 when there is no association between the independent and the dependent variable. For binary variables, it can be expressed as follows:

$$e^{\beta Z} = \frac{\frac{Prob(Y=1)}{(1-Prob(Y=1))}(Z=1)}{\frac{Prob(Y=1)}{(1-Prob(Y=1))}(Z=0)} \quad (3.2)$$

Results show that the domain name's age effect is positive and statistically significant, thus increasing the probability of exporting. An English version being available on the website is the feature that most contributes to inferring the export orientation, being associated with a high OR. Similarly, presence of export-related keywords is also connected to the export orientation since it significantly raises the probability of exporting. The model performs relatively well, as pointed out by the pseudo-R^2 (0.534), the high prediction accuracy (81.4%) and the Hosmer-Lemeshow test which, in this case, indicates that the model is adequate to explain the data. Table 3.5 shows the model prediction performance by comparing the firm's actual export orientation to the predictions made by this model.

Table 3.4: Prediction of export orientation with manually retrieved WWW variables

Variables	β	SE	p-value	OR
DOM_AGE_i	0.068	0.039	0.083	1.070
EN_i	2.186	0.333	0.000	8.901
$KEYWORDS_i$	1.203	0.311	0.000	3.329
$(Constant)$	-1.717	0.489	0.000	0.180
Pseudo-R^2	0.534			
Hosmer-Lemeshow	0.112			
Prediction accuracy	81.4%			

Notes: The null hypothesis of the Hosmer and Lemeshow test is that the model is fit. The industry dummies have been included in the model specification.

Table 3.5: Comparison of the model predicting business export orientation from manually retrieved website features to the actual export orientation of the firm

Export orientation	$MANUAL = 0$	$MANUAL = 1$
$EXPORT = 0$	44.6%	11.4%
$EXPORT = 1$	7.1%	36.9%

The results of this model were compared with the prediction performance of the baseline model, which included the firms' structural variables and was made up as follows:

$$Prob(EXPORT_i = 1) = \frac{e^{W_i}}{1 + e^{W_i}};$$

$$W_i = \beta_0 + \beta_1 SIZE_i + \beta_2 LP_i + \beta_3 AGE_i + \gamma INDUSTRY_i, \tag{3.3}$$

where β_0 is a constant and the coefficients β_1, β_2, β_3 and γ indicate the relative influence of each feature on the prediction of the category of the dependent variable. The estimations for this model are reported in Table 3.6. The effect of the three considered variables is positive and statistically significant, thus contributing to the probability of being an exporter. This model

also performs relatively well, with a pseudo-R^2 of 0.468, a prediction accuracy
of 77.7% and a good data fit according to the Hosmer-Lemeshow test results.
When comparing both models, it can be stated that the web-based variables
contain as much information about a firm's export orientation as the firm's
size, age and labor productivity. Table 3.7 summarizes the model prediction
performance by comparing the actual export orientation of the firm to the
predictions made by this model.

Table 3.6: Prediction of export orientation with firm structural variables

Variables	β	SE	p-value	OR
$SIZE_i$	0.847	0.178	0.000	2.333
LP_i	0.016	0.006	0.016	1.016
AGE_i	0.058	0.015	0.000	1.060
$(Constant)$	-3.556	0.604	0.000	0.029
Pseudo-R^2	0.468			
Hosmer-Lemeshow	0.658			
Prediction accuracy	77.7%			

Notes: The null hypothesis of the Hosmer and Lemeshow test is that the model is fit. The
industry dummies have been included in the model specification.

Table 3.7: Comparison of the model predicting business export orientation
from firm structural variables to the actual export orientation of the firm

Export orientation	$BASELINE = 0$	$BASELINE = 1$
$EXPORT = 0$	40.3%	11.6%
$EXPORT = 1$	11.0%	37.1%

3.4 Automating the retrieval of web-based variables

This section describes the method which was followed to obtain the export
orientation indicator built from automatic web-based variables, as well as the
evaluation of their performance. To do so, we first describe the implementation of a web data mining tool to automatically obtain information from

corporate websites, and second, the statistical techniques applied to construct the automatic web-based variables. Finally, we describe the replication of the manual web-based model with the automatic web-based variables, which was done to check their predictive power.

3.4.1 Architecture of the web data mining system for analyzing corporate websites

To automatically extract and analyze the contents from the corporate websites, we extended the web mining model presented in Domenech et al. (2012) with specific analysis modules. Figure 3.1 shows the architecture of this system, which consists of three main modules: the **capture module**, the **analysis module** and the **production module**.

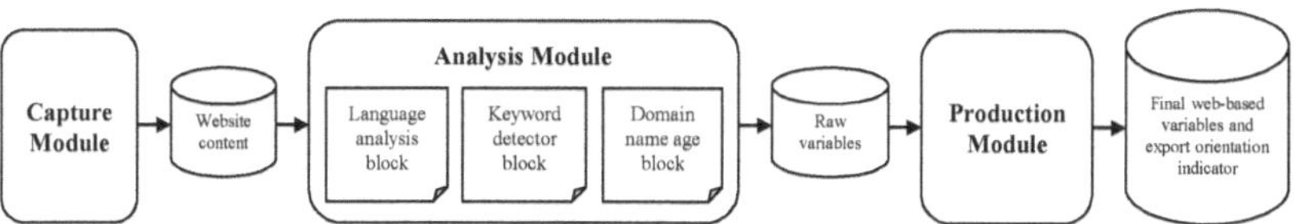

Figure 3.1: Model for a web data mining system to retrieve the web-based variables

The capture module basically acts as a crawler that parses and downloads all the website contents from the corporate sites provided as input. It has been implemented as a modified version of HTTrack (Roche, 2014), which is a robot that recursively parses and downloads the links found in the initial URI.

The analysis module examines the contents downloaded by the capture module to produce some raw variables that potentially relate to the firm's economic variable under study; i.e., the export orientation in this case. This module is composed of several independent blocks, each one computing related variables.

The *language analysis block* detects the language in which every HTML file on the site is written. Its output is the number of resources in each considered language. The *keyword detector block* departs from a list of keywords and counts the number of occurrences of each keyword in the text of the website. It provides counting not only for strict matching (i.e., exact coincidence), but also for wide matching, that is, derived words are also considered a coincidence. The *domain name age block* makes a request to a *whois* server to find the date on which the provided domain name was registered.

Finally, the production module takes as input all the raw variables generated by the analysis module to compute the web-based variables for detecting, in this study case, the export orientation of firms. For this purpose, statistical methods to estimate the probability of exporting given the raw variables were used. More details on these methods are provided below.

3.4.2 Construction and validation of automatic web-based variables

The web-based model described in Section 3.3.3 relied on two website features that were manually retrieved (EN_i and $KEYWORDS_i$). This section describes the supervised learning methods applied to estimate the manually retrieved variables from the raw variables generated by the analysis module of the system. These methods, which are particularly useful with big data, bring up much more realistic prediction performance measures (in terms of obtaining good out-of-sample predictions) than other measures generally used in economics (Varian, 2014).

English version The detection of the foreign language version of the website from the related raw variables (number of HTML documents in each language) relied on the ratio of documents in the foreign language (English) to the number of documents in the local language (Spanish). The rationale behind this is that the English version can be functional, although not all the website's sections are translated.

One of the limitations of our capture module is its ability for detecting duplicate content. This makes that the number of apparently different documents grows uncontrollably with some dynamic websites. This happens, for instance, when two (or more) different terms in an HTML form lead to the same page. To alleviate this problem, a saturation parameter was included. It was defined as the maximum number of files to be considered in each language so that the number of documents saturates at this level.

Both the language ratio and saturation threshold parameters were tuned by a 10-fold cross-validation method. This method assesses in which way the results of a particular statistical analysis would generalize to an independent data set. Basically, this method involves splitting the data sample into a number of complementary subsets, then performing the analysis on one subset (referred to as the *training set*) and validating it on the other subsets (referred to as the *test set*). In this case, 10 partitions were made, so that 10 rounds of cross-validation were performed (to reduce variability in the test error estimation). With this method, we were able to choose the values for both parameters that led to the lower test error, thus limiting the problem of overfitting.

The results of this method are shown in Figure 3.2. The saturation threshold varied from 1 to 40 documents, while the language ratio ranged from 0.1 to 2.0. However, for the sake of clarity, the figure shows only a few of these values. The results indicate that the optimal value for the saturation threshold is 11 HTML files, while the optimal value for the language ratio is 0.4. These parameter values were used to compute the estimated *EN* variable.

When compared to the manually retrieved variable, the estimated one (EN_i^A) provides an overall prediction accuracy of 84.3%, as Table 3.8 shows. A detailed analysis of the classification errors reveals that false positives occur when some error messages are found in the HTML text (generated by the web server). False negatives are found to be usually caused by crawling errors (i.e., not all the pages are downloaded). In captured information terms, the moderate correlation found between both variables (0.676) shows that the estimated variable contains similar information to the manually retrieved one.

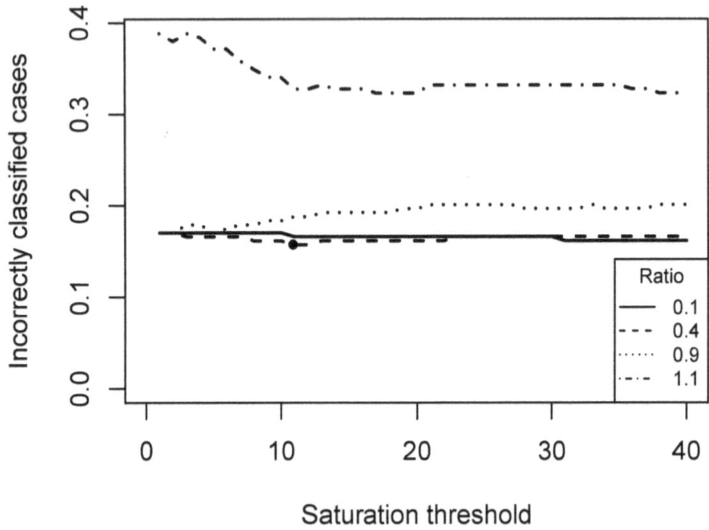

Figure 3.2: Cross-validation test error for a range of parameter values of the
automatic English version indicator

Table 3.8: Prediction performance of the automatic English version indicator

English version	$AUTO = 0$	$AUTO = 1$
$MANUAL = 0$	50.7%	8.3%
$MANUAL = 1$	7.4%	33.6%

Presence of export-related keywords   The automatic variable for export-
related keywords ($KEYWORDS_i^A$) was built from the raw features that included the number of occurrences that apply strict and wide matching algorithms to each word in the list of terms. This list consisted of the same
keywords related to business exports as the ones used in the manual model.
Though these raw variables are numeric variables that doubtlessly include
valuable information, they were transformed into binary in order to replicate
the manual variable and thus checking the validity of their automatic extrac-

tion, as it is one of our objectives. Since the number of features was large, the Least Absolute Shrinkage and Selection Operator (LASSO) method was employed to find a more parsimonious model. The LASSO, which is derived from the Elastic Net Regression method, is a statistical method for variable selection which includes a penalty term (shrinkage parameter) and works by producing regressions where some coefficients are set at zero. Hence, problems such as multicollinearity are limited feasibly. The shrinkage parameter (λ) required by this method was tuned by a 10-fold cross-validation procedure, whose results are presented in Figure 3.3. This procedure resulted in the selection of a logistic regression model with 15 features to be used to estimate the presence of the export-related keywords. That is, 15 binary variables that take a value of 1 when a match with a given word in the resulting list occurs.

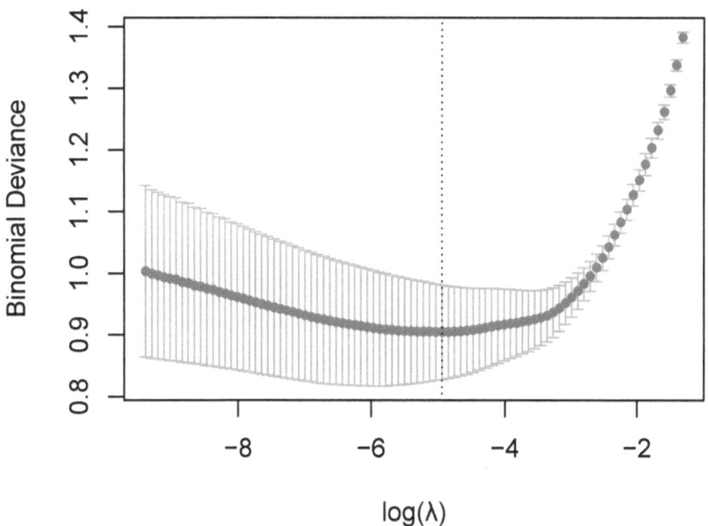

Figure 3.3: Cross-validation test error (with 5% confidence intervals) for a range of λ parameter values of the LASSO Method for computing the automatic *KEYWORDS* indicator

The prediction performance of the estimated indicator ($KEYWORDS_i^A$)
is summarized in Table 3.9. As observed, the proposed method works relatively well since the prediction accuracy is 85.1%. Most misclassifications
come from false negatives, which are found in 13.1% of corporate websites. A
more detailed analysis reveals that most of these false negatives are due to
the incomplete crawling of the site. In captured information terms, the strong
correlation found between both variables (0.714) indicates that the estimated
variable contains similar information to the manually retrieved one.

Table 3.9: Prediction performance of the automatic $KEYWORDS$ indicator

$KEYWORDS$	$AUTO = 0$	$AUTO = 1$
$MANUAL = 0$	52.8%	1.7%
$MANUAL = 1$	13.1%	32.3%

3.4.3 Predicting firm export orientation from automatic web-based variables

The automatic export-related variables EN_i^A and $KEYWORDS_i^A$ computed
in the previous section are now employed to finally estimate the business export
orientation. To do so, the manually retrieved variables used in the manual
web-based model are replaced with the automatically retrieved ones.

The results for the estimation of this model are reported in Table 3.10. This
model attempts to capture most of the prediction accuracy achieved with the
manual web-based model. The estimation results of this new model give a
prediction accuracy of 78.2%, which is slightly below the 81.4% resulting from
the manual web-based model. Taking into account that the model based in
manually retrieved web variables acts as an upper bound of the prediction performance of the automatic model, this result means that 96% of the prediction
power of the manual model has been successfully reproduced. For each variable effect, in this case the domain name's age and presence of export-related
keywords are not statistically significant. The English version variable remains

Table 3.10: Prediction of export orientation with automatically retrieved WWW variables

Variable	β	SE	p-value	OR
DOM_AGE_i	0.050	0.046	0.274	1.052
EN_i^A	1.888	0.379	0.000	6.604
$KEYWORDS_i^A$	0.541	0.379	0.152	1.718
$(Constant)$	-1.721	0.652	0.008	0.179
Pseudo-R^2	0.481			
Hosmer-Lemeshow	0.732			
Prediction accuracy	78.2%			

Notes: The null hypothesis of the Hosmer and Lemeshow test is that the model is fit. The industry dummies have been included in the model specification.

statistically significant, and is associated with an OR of 6.6. This model also performs relatively well, as pointed out by the pseudo-R^2 (0.481), the high prediction accuracy mentioned above and the Hosmer-Lemeshow test, which indicates that the model correctly fits the data.

Table 3.11 shows the model performance by comparing the firm's actual export orientation to the predictions made by this model. A detailed comparison of the results of the manual and automatic web-based models (see Tables 3.5 and 3.11) evidences that, as expected, the main difference lies in the false negative rate (7.1% vs. 10.0%), which derives from limitations in website crawling. Overall, the comparison shows that the automatic variables are good predictors of firms' export orientation, despite losing some performance if compared to the manually retrieved ones.

Table 3.11: Comparison of the model predicting business export orientation from automatically retrieved website features to the actual export orientation of the firm

Export orientation	$AUTO = 0$	$AUTO = 1$
$EXPORT = 0$	38.0%	11.8%
$EXPORT = 1$	10.0%	40.2%

3.5 Conclusions

The online data stream increases on a daily basis as people and companies
adopt and use the Internet and web technologies. Corporate websites, which
are being widely adopted by any kind of firm, reflect the intentions and activities of companies. Following the Big Data paradigm, they can be used as a
source of information to produce real-time indicators of the evolution of some
economic variables. This is particularly important given that the availability
of fresh and frequent data about the economy gives governments more time
to react and correct imbalances. As use of web technologies and their economic and social importance are fully expanding, more granular and updated
information is available and also demanded at the same time.

This paper has explored the use of Big Data analysis on corporate websites
for nowcasting firms' export orientation by automatically producing a web-
based indicator. This objective has been accomplished in two steps: first, by
finding the corporate website features related to the firms' export orientation;
second, by implementing and validating the automatic extraction of these
features through a web data mining system.

Our results show that the selected website features contain as much information about the export orientation of companies as the main firm's structural
variables (size, age and labor productivity). In contrast to the classic variables
obtained from official sources, which are usually made available with long de-
lays, these web features can be retrieved and analyzed in real time. Moreover,
our system for automatically analyzing corporate websites achieved 96% of the
prediction accuracy of the model with manually retrieved web features, thus
validating a new inexpensive and timely source of information about individual
firm's export orientation.

From the academic point of view, these web-based variables can complement firms' data from other sources to understand the role played by corporate
websites in the internationalization strategy. The results of this study also
have implications for policymakers, particularly for the evaluation of export
promotion policies. By demonstrating that there are website features from

which export indicators can be built, a new way for timely and inexpensive monitoring opens. As their retrieval has been automated, the continuous monitoring of export orientation is now possible. This would allow policymakers to detect how fast companies are reacting to some export promotion policies or what the trend in trade openness is, among others. Furthermore, as website contents are usually related to the designed corporate strategy, it is expected that the decision to export is reflected earlier on the website than in foreign sales, thus anticipating future exports.

There are some limitations of the study that are worth mentioning. First, caution should be taken when generalizing the implications beyond the scope of this study. The results come from only a sample of firms from the Region of Valencia, in east Spain, so they may be specific to this setting, particularly those variables related to language. Further studies using samples from other regions and countries should be carried out. Second, only cross-sectional data are analyzed. A longitudinal analysis would help determine how fast changes in export behavior translate into website changes.

Given the system's ability to retrieve a large number of website features in a short period of time, and the advantages and possibilities offered by web technology, in future works we will explore the relation between other website features and exports, and with other business activities.

Chapter 4

Monitoring e-commerce adoption from online data

Chapter 4 is an adapted version of this published research paper:

- Title: Monitoring e-commerce adoption from online data
- Authors: Desamparados Blazquez, Josep Domenech, Jose A. Gil and Ana Pont
- Year of publication: 2018
- Journal: Knowledge and Information Systems
- Volume: Online (pending to assign volume)
- DOI: 10.1007/s10115-018-1233-7

92

4.1 Introduction

Internet and the WWW (the Web) have emerged as the main drivers of the
transition into the digital society and economy, transforming day by day our
lifestyle and habits. This is particularly relevant and challenging for companies, which are enforced to adapt to the new way of doing business that this
digital context implies. Indeed, with the empowering influence of the Internet,
the Web has turned into much more than a window for firms to show their
products and services to the world. Nowadays, firms can use their websites as
commercial platforms by engaging in electronic commerce (e-commerce).

More and more firms are adopting e-commerce because of the great advantages and new opportunities that it involves. For instance, it helps firms to reduce costs, be closer to the clients and provide a more customized service (Sohrabi et al., 2012). In addition, engaging in e-commerce encourages the adoption of other innovations, such as electronic exchange data systems or automated inventory management (Ordanini and Rubera, 2010; Shih, 2012). For all these reasons, the global B2C e-commerce market is in expansion. In 2015, B2C e-commerce sales worldwide reached up to nearly €2.3 trillion, which represents an increase of about 20% with respect to the previous year and a contribution of 3.1% to the global gross domestic product (Ecommerce Foundation, 2016).

To promote and monitor the evolution of the digital economy, governments require detailed and updated information about the level of adoption of e-commerce in firms, grouped by different economic sectors and geographic areas. The information about the current e-commerce adoption, evolution and trends help them to better define strategic plans for the economy and enact laws for regulating this activity (Oliveira and Martins, 2010; Rodríguez-Ardura and Meseguer-Artola, 2010).

In fact, private and public institutions are aware of the value of these data so that they are making efforts to monitor e-commerce evolution. The national and supranational statistics offices and other e-commerce observers currently obtain these data using surveys (Eurostat, 2016; INE, 2016; ONS, 2016). This traditional method that turns to primary sources bring truthful information, but the procedure implies a number of disadvantages (Griffis et al., 2003; Peytchev, 2013; Bulligan et al., 2015). First, the processing costs are high considering the human resources involved. Second, the generally low response rate complicates the characterization of the variables under study, potentially introduces bias and leads to higher survey costs and complexity in terms of design, implementation and data processing. The time taken by this data processing makes surveys inappropriate to conduct a short-term monitoring of the economy, which is more important than ever in the Digital Era because changes happen fast.

To deal with the shortcomings mentioned above, there is an increasing tendency to use online data which, appropriately extracted and processed, can result in accurate and prompt indicators for a variety of economic topics, ranging from unemployment to car sales or export orientation (Choi and Varian, 2012; Vicente et al., 2015; Blazquez and Domenech, 2018b). Online data show some advantages compared to traditional sources of information when generating economic indicators, as pointed out by Edelman (2012) and Einav and Levin (2014). These include: very fast processing times because of their electronic nature; a high level of granularity; lower collection costs; and the availability of an enormous quantity of fresh information because people, business and governments generate and share information online every minute of the day.

This digitized and huge amount of information, increasingly known as "Big Data", imply challenges for computation and statistics, such as data storage and processing scalability, noise aggregation or spurious correlations (Fan et al., 2014). For these reasons, Big Data requires specifically-developed computational and statistical techniques ("Big Analytics") that allow their appropriate exploitation, in real time and more efficiently than traditional methods would (Einav and Levin, 2014; Pokorný et al., 2015; Blazquez and Domenech, 2018a).

In this vein, this paper proposes a Big Data approach to generate an indicator for e-commerce adoption from the analysis of information provided by corporate websites. In order to make the information retrieval process from these sources quick and feasible, we have designed and implemented the System for Automatically Monitoring E-commerce Adoption (SAME), which is an intelligent system aimed at automatically capturing and processing economic related data from websites by making use of web scraping techniques and learning methods for Big Data. The final output of the system is the e-commerce adoption indicator, which is produced by means of a classification model in which more than 150 features extracted from websites were included.

The system performance has been evaluated with a sample of 426 corporate websites of manufacturing firms based in France and Spain, which were manually classified. Results show that SAME manages to predict the availability of e-commerce activity with a precision about 91%. A more detailed analysis evidenced that, as expected, websites with e-commerce tend to include some specific keywords and have a private area. The automatic nature of the proposal enables a large scale monitoring of the economy, providing prompt and actual information to governments and organizations.

The remainder of this paper is organized as follows. Section 4.2 reviews the literature on the generation of economic indicators from online data. Section 4.3 describes the architecture of the system developed for monitoring e-commerce availability on corporate websites. Section 4.4 describes the experimental results, including an overview of the data and a comprehensive analysis of the classification model performance. Finally, Section 4.5 draws some concluding remarks.

4.2 Related work

The generation of economic indicators from Internet activity is an incipient research topic that is receiving increasing attention due to the potential relation between online data and offline phenomena (Jungherr and Jürgens, 2013). Although the first attempts in this direction date back to 2009, it is in the last couple of years when the potential of online information for monitoring the economy is being revealed. Indeed, Einav and Levin (2014) suggest that economic indicators from automatically gathered online data may already be more reliable than government survey measures in some countries. To deal with such amount of digitized data, the application of Big Data retrieval and analysis techniques is being increasingly required (Varian, 2014; Pokorný et al., 2015).

There exist some different research lines that explore the generation of economic indicators from Internet data. One of these lines is focused in relating the popularity of some keyword searches (generally obtained from *Google Trends* reports) to the evolution of specific economic magnitudes. In this vein, the seminal work by Choi and Varian (2009b) analyzed how some search categories in Google were related to car and home sales and to income tourists. Later, the same authors proposed a model for nowcasting the initial claims for unemployment in the US labor market by including the popularity of some specific category searches in the prediction model (Choi and Varian, 2012). Similar approaches have been considered for predicting unemployment-related variables in other countries, such as France (Fondeur and Karamé, 2013) and Spain (Vicente et al., 2015), as well as for predicting other economic-related variables (Hand and Judge, 2012). However, search engines are not the only online source for Internet-based economic indicators. For instance, social network activities have been used as a predictor of the evolution of the stock market (Bollen et al., 2011; Arias et al., 2013), box office revenues (Kulkarni et al., 2012; Kim et al., 2015) or telecom sales (Bughin, 2015).

Corporate websites are also a rich source of information for monitoring what is happening in the economy, since companies usually reflect new products and intended strategies on them. Furthermore, the digital and public nature of the Web makes it possible to automatically analyze websites and generate economic indicators from them (Domenech et al., 2012). However, websites contain a large volume of unstructured information which requires from Big Data retrieval and analysis methods such as web scraping and penalized regressions. Web scraping is a retrieval technique that consists in collecting and processing information from the Web, so that it can be used for further analysis (Munzert et al., 2015). Then, some computational statistics techniques should be applied in order to reduce the information dimensionality and produce accurate economic indicators. These include the penalized regression LASSO (which will be described later), classification and regression trees (CART), neural nets or support vector machines (Hastie et al., 2009; Varian, 2014). In this context, Youtie et al. (2012) and Arora et al. (2013) applied web scraping and content analysis techniques on corporate websites to track company strategies on emerging technology sectors, while Li et al. (2016) tracked firms' sales growth. Similarly, Blazquez and Domenech (2014) described how website contents are connected to the firm export orientation, and how this information can be used to automatically monitor the export orientation of an economy (Blazquez and Domenech, 2018b).

The permanent interest of statistics offices in monitoring the adoption of e-commerce (Eurostat, 2016; INE, 2016; ONS, 2016) demonstrates that its development is one of the aspects of the digital economy that receives important attention from policymakers. Indeed, the work conducted by the Italian National Statistics Institute (Istat) constitutes a precedent on the detection of e-commerce and other web functionalities by analyzing websites. Their proposal Barcaroli et al. (2014, 2015) relies on content analysis on scraped websites to detect e-commerce availability (B2B and B2C indistinctly), obtaining an accuracy about 85%. With respect to this initial study, our proposal constitutes an alternative approach in which not only text content is analyzed, but also the HTML source, the HTTP headers and the website structure are considered to detect and quantify a number of features potentially related to e-commerce (e.g. having a private area or outlinks to external sites such as payment gateways). This way, not only the accuracy could be improved (up to 91%), but also our proposal contributes to shed light on which website features are indeed related to e-commerce implementation.

Currently, most of the research efforts on e-commerce are mainly focused on developing the technology to run these sites. For instance, user behavior patterns are being explored with web usage mining techniques to make e-commerce sites more profitable by including recommendation systems (He, 2012; Rosaci and Sarnè, 2014; Zhao et al., 2016) or improving site responsiveness (Poggi et al., 2014; Hao et al., 2013; Suchacka and Borzemski, 2013).

E-commerce sites have also been studied to detect its success factors. In this context, by doing a manual analysis of the sites or conducting surveys to the managers, characteristics such as the design (Hasan, 2016), website quality (Lee and Kozar, 2006), navigability (Hernández et al., 2009) and ease of purchase processing (Zhang et al., 2011) are found to be determinant for the successful adoption of an e-commerce strategy.

A different approach is followed by Thorleuchter and Van den Poel (2012), who apply text mining techniques to build a prediction model on the success of e-commerce companies. Similarly, Stoll and Hepp (2013) proposes a technique that analyzes HTML tag attributes of e-commerce sites to discover which of the six most popular e-commerce systems is being used. Unfortunately, all the reviewed works depart from the existence of an e-commerce site, thus being inappropriate for monitoring the adoption of e-commerce by any firm.

4.3   SAME: a system for detecting and monitoring e-commerce adoption

This section describes the architecture of SAME, the intelligent system developed for automatically detecting and monitoring e-commerce availability. SAME follows a web content mining approach (as defined by Cooley et al. (1997)) to extract and analyze data from the selected corporate websites, and finally compute the e-commerce adoption indicator. Figure 4.1 shows the architecture of SAME, which consists of three main modules, each one implementing one of the web mining tasks described by Kosala and Blockeel (2000). These are: the capture module (resource finding), the analysis module (information selection and pre-processing), and the production module (generalization). Below, we describe how these modules were implemented.

4.3.1   The capture module

The **capture module** is the part of the system that is in charge of accessing, downloading and storing the corporate websites of the firms under analysis, which are provided as input. These websites provides us with three types of information that will be used to feed the analysis module. The first is the text content included in the HTML (or Adobe Flash SWF) resources, since companies usually describe there the activities carried out by them. The second is the HTML (or Adobe Flash SWF) code itself, as long as it includes important information about the structure and organization of the website.

This includes, for instance, the URLs in the links and anchor elements or the forms to access the ordering process. Relevant keywords may appear both

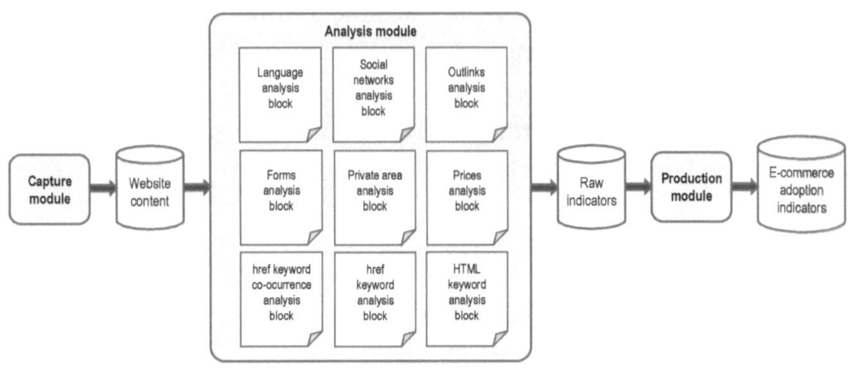

Figure 4.1: Architecture of SAME

in the text content and in parts of the HTML attributes. The third type of
information is the HTTP headers issued by the web server in the responses of
the communication protocol, because they contain information about how to
interpret the resource (e.g. Content-Type, Content-Language, etc.).

This module acts basically scraping the Web and it is implemented as
a modified version of HTTrack (Roche, 2014), which is an open source web
crawler that downloads a website by recursively following the links found on
the resources. HTTrack provides certain support for discovering and interpreting hyperlinks in the *javascript* code, as well as for parsing Adobe Flash
SWF content, both of which are relatively common technologies in corporate
websites. This allows us to follow some links that are not included in the
HTML anchor tags, thus enabling a more comprehensive crawling and analysis. This module is capable of dealing with redirections, both at the HTTP
and HTML level. And, also, it permits to store the response headers sent by
the web server in the HTTP interactions.

In addition, this module is respectful with the companies' web servers. It
respects the directives of the robots exclusion standard (i.e., *robots.txt*) so that
only those websites which give permission to be crawled are actually down-

loaded and stored. The crawler is also configured to use a limited bandwidth and download time on each website to avoid overloading the servers because of our research.

Finally, this module is equipped with a version control system implemented with *git* in order to store snapshots of the websites at different moments of time. Although this feature is not used in the experiments presented below, it is potentially useful, as it would allow us to track firm behavior changes through time by comparing different versions of the same website.

4.3.2 The analysis module

The **analysis module** examines and processes the content previously down-loaded by the capture model to produce multiple raw features that are expected to be related to the firm's e-commerce availability. This module is composed of several independent blocks that parallelly compute raw website features potentially related to e-commerce. Blocks are implemented as independent scripts, each one using selected technologies for their purpose, providing flexibility to the implementation and making it easy to parellelize and distribute the tasks. Most blocks are implemented by using python and shell scripting, complemented with other command-line tools such as *sed*. Parallelization was carried out by means of the Distributed Parallel Processing Shell Script (PPSS). These blocks are the following:

- **Forms analysis block:** It is in charge of detecting the presence and number of forms, both in HTML and XHTML format, in a website. It is implemented by detecting the <form> element in the source file.

- **Private area analysis block:** It is set to find website areas restricted to registered users only. To do so, the block focuses on discovering forms with password fields inside them.

- **Prices analysis block:** It is designed to detect the presence of currency symbols (e.g., £, \$, €) or abbreviations (e.g., GBP, USD, EUR) close to numeric characters, since this is usually indicative of the presence of prices in a website, and thus closely related to e-commerce services.

- **HTML keyword analysis block:** This block takes a list of e-commerce related keywords and counts the number of occurrences of each keyword in the text of the website. This list included terms such as: *tienda*, shop, *carro*, *panier*, cart or purchase. The block provides counting not only for strict matching (i.e., exact coincidence), but also for wide matching, which is performed by applying a word stemmer to the website text contents. Therefore, the block can also detect derived words departing from the stem of the given keywords or other words related to them. The derived words may be also helpful to detect e-commerce activity.

- **Href keyword analysis block:** It works in a way similar to the HTML keyword detector block with strict matching, but applied to the link in the *href* of an HTML anchor tag. E-commerce sites usually include words related to the ordering process in the links.

- **Href keyword co-occurrence analysis block:** This block counts the number of terms related to e-commerce that appear in the *href* property of an HTML anchor tag. In this way, the e-commerce sites that use processing links intensively are detected.

- **Social networks analysis block:** It is in charge of detecting whether the sites include links to some of the most widespread social network sites, including Facebook, Twitter, Google+, LinkedIn, Youtube, Vimeo, Flickr and Reddit. Its implementation analyzes the <a> elements in the source files.

- **Outlinks analysis block:** It analyzes the HTML resources of each website in order to find references that link the contents to other external sites, such as banks, payment gateways and so on.

- **Language analysis block:** It detects the language in which the HTML resources of the corporate websites are written. Its output is the number of HTML resources in each language, being French, Spanish and English the most relevant ones in the experiments presented below.

4.3.3 The production module

Finally, the **production module** takes as input all the raw features generated by the analysis module to compute the web-based indicator for e-commerce availability. This module implements some learning methods to build the classification model for detecting e-commerce availability and to properly treat the training data. The implementation was done using the free statistical software R (R Core Team, 2015).

To build the classification model, the LASSO (Least Absolute Shrinkage and Selection Operator) regularization was applied to a logistic regression model that takes all the raw features (more than 150) as input. Logistic regression is a linear classifier that models the probability of the response variable (binary or with multiple categories) taking a particular value, and generates predictions based on the fitted probabilities (James et al., 2013; Kuhn and Johnson, 2013). In the case of this study, the logistic regression models the probability that a firm is enrolled in e-commerce. The LASSO, developed by Tibshirani (1996), is a regularization method for regression models which is used to find more parsimonious models, that is, to reduce the number of variables without losing predictive performance. To do so, it includes a shrinkage parameter (λ) that makes some of the variable coefficients take value zero, thus allowing variable selection. In this study, this parameter is adjusted by means of a 10-fold cross-validation and it is selected following the "one standard error rule" (Hastie et al., 2013). This rule allows to select the most parsimonious model whose error is within one standard error of the best model's error. The LASSO is generally applied when the number of predictors is large and/or when some of them are highly correlated, given its ability to identify the most important variables and select among redundant predictors. As a result, not only more parsimonious models can be built, but also multicollinearity can be feasibly limited (Tibshirani, 1996; Hastie et al., 2009). Given its ability to reduce the dimensionality of information, it is a particularly useful technique for analyzing the huge volume of online data that is being generated day by day in a Big Data context (Varian, 2014).

About the training process of the classification model in this module, it is important to remark that it should be done with a balanced sample otherwise it would compromise the learning process (Menardi and Torelli, 2014). A sample is balanced when each of the categories (or classes) of the variable under study (i.e., e-commerce availability in this case) is present in the same proportion. This way, the model is trained to be equally successful for detecting e-commerce presence or absence. The production module balances the training data by employing a method which generates new observations of the minority class (usually, websites with e-commerce) and under-samples the majority class.

4.4 Experimental results

4.4.1 Data

The evaluation of the system was performed by applying the predictive model to 426 corporate websites from manufacturing companies[1] based in France and Spain. The list of corporate websites was randomly retrieved from the SABI and ORBIS databases, which are provided by the company Bureau van Dijk. To perform the supervised learning process, we firstly did a manual revision of each website in order to detect the presence or absence of an e-commerce platform. This feature, which is the dependent variable in the predictive model, was coded as a binary variable with value 1 if the website had an e-commerce platform available. Then, the list of websites was provided as input for the capture module of SAME, which retrieved 21.9 GB representing

---

[1] Companies with codes 10-33 in the Statistical Classification of Economic Activities in the European Community NACE Rev. 2 (Eurostat, 2008).

741,350 resources. After that, the analysis module processed the 426 websites to generate for each of them all the raw features (161 in total), from which the classification model for e-commerce availability selects the more relevant and is built. For descriptive purposes, they have been assembled as follows:

- **Forms:** Feature that is coded as a binary variable with value 1 if the website contained any HTML or XHTML form, and 0 otherwise.

- **Private area:** Feature that is coded as a binary variable with value 1 if there was a private area available and 0 otherwise.

- **Prices:** Feature that is coded as a binary variable with value 1 if there were product prices available on the website and 0 otherwise.

- **HTML Keywords:** This group of features make reference to the detection of keywords related to e-commerce on the HTML documents of the corporate website. A list of about 45 keywords was prepared and then searched for by SAME on the HTML documents. For each keyword and match type (which included strict and wide matching), the system coded a binary variable with value 1 if there was at least one coincidence on the website HTMLs and 0 otherwise. As a result, about 80 variables were obtained.

- **Href Keywords:** This group of features make reference to the detection of keywords related to e-commerce on the href attribute of the anchor tags of the corporate website HTMLs. The above-mentioned list of keywords was searched for by SAME on the website links, taking into account only the strict matching. For each keyword, a binary variable with value 1 was coded if there was at least one coincidence on the website links and 0 otherwise. As a result, about 45 binary variables were obtained.

- **Href Keyword Co-occurrence:** This feature is related to the intensity in which the keywords appear in the HTML anchor tags. It is coded as a binary variable with value 1 if the website contained links whose href included at least two keywords of the above-mentioned list, and 0 otherwise.

- **Social networks:** Feature that refers to the presence or absence of links to any of the social networks explored by the *social networks analysis block* in the capture module of SAME. It is coded as a binary variable with value 1 if the website contained any link to a social network and 0 otherwise.

- **Outlinks:** Feature that is coded as a binary variable with value 1 if the website contained any link to external sources and 0 otherwise.

- **Language availability:** This group of features refer to the different language versions of the website that are available. The languages that have been considered are Spanish and French, because they are the native languages of the firms in the sample, and English because it is the most common language for international transactions. For this reason, this group is composed of three particular features, which are coded as three binary variables with value 1 if the website had any HTML in Spanish, French or English, respectively, and 0 otherwise.

4.4.2   Results

This section firstly shows some descriptive statistics that were obtained to provide a general view of the presence of the selected features on both groups of websites (with and without e-commerce). Second, the predictive model for the e-commerce availability is built by using the learning methods previously discussed. Finally, some graphical representations of the results are provided to illustrate how the model works.

4.4.2.1   Overview

A first approach is to explore whether or not the presence of some features differed substantially between the corporate websites with and without e-commerce. These differences are illustrated in Table 4.1, which also shows

that the sample is unbalanced, since 60 firms offered e-commerce services
while the remaining 366 did not. Regarding the presence of features, the majority of them were more frequently found in the websites of firms with some
e-commerce capabilities, as expected.

Table 4.1: Presence of key features on e-commerce and non e-commerce websites

Feature	Mean e-commerce=1 (N=60)	Mean e-commerce=0 (N=366)
Forms	0.950	0.699
Private area	0.583	0.153
Prices	0.600	0.167
CK Ordering	0.983	0.861
CK Products	0.750	0.402
CK Other processes	0.833	0.664
LK Ordering	0.850	0.385
LK Products	0.850	0.680
LK Other processes	0.317	0.022
LK Co-occurrence	0.517	0.139
Social networks	0.550	0.257
Outlinks	0.983	0.869
French version	0.767	0.440
Spanish version	0.317	0.642
English version	0.400	0.413

Notes: Keyword-related features have been grouped by topic and target area (content keywords, CK; or link keywords, LK).

A closer look to the differences reveals interesting patterns that will be
useful in the classification model. For instance, it is shown that almost every
website with e-commerce includes at least one HTML form, being also more
frequent on them compared to those websites without e-commerce (95% vs.
69.9%). This could be related to the fact that forms are usually involved in
online ordering, although they can also be used as a simple contact method.
The private area exhibits a similar pattern (58.3% vs. 15.3%) since many e-
commerce websites require customers to log in to gain access to the ordering

or product browsing functionalities. Analogously, product prices are more frequently detected when websites include e-commerce services (60% vs. 16.7%).

About the features related to the presence of keywords, they have been presented in Table 4.1 under three main topic areas ("Ordering process", "Products or services offered" and "Other actions, such as payment, delivery and refund"), and also divided into content matching (CK, which include the HMTL keywords) and link matching (LK, which include the href keywords). As expected, the presence of all these groups of features was greater in the set of websites with e-commerce than in those without it. Notice that these groups were prepared for illustrative purposes only and they are not inputs for the classification model introduced below.

This descriptive analysis has helped to confirm that some of the considered features are effectively related to e-commerce and the majority of their values meet our initial expectations. These features appear, in general more frequently in websites that offer e-commerce facilities with respect to those that do not offer them. In order to determine which features are more useful to detect the presence of e-commerce, tests of statistical inference have been conducted. These tests are shown in the next section.

4.4.2.2 The classification model

After exploring the features that mainly differ between e-commerce and non e-commerce websites, this section evaluates the classification performance of SAME after training the production module as described above.

At this point, it is important to remark that to properly evaluate the model, it is recommended to conduct a holdout process where the sample is split into two parts: a training set and a test set. The first set is used to train the model, so that it learns how to work, while the second is used to evaluate it (including the classification accuracy and any other result). The evaluation of the model with a different set from the one which is used to build it brings a much more reliable approach to the real performance of the model, making it possible to generalize the results (Hastie et al., 2009). From the different

split ratios that are proposed in the literature, in this study it was applied the
75-25 one, in which 75% of the observations set up the training set while the
remaining 25% form the test set.

To prepare the training set, 75% of the observations (i.e., 320 websites)
were randomly hold out from the sample. Following the distribution of the
initial sample, in which only 14% of the websites have e-commerce, this set is
also unbalanced (45 websites with e-commerce vs. 275 without). That is, one
of the categories of the variable under study is over-represented. Since building
a robust predictive model requires a balanced training sample, the SMOTE
method (Chawla et al., 2002) was applied to the training set. This method
artificially generates new observations of the minority class using their nearest
neighbors and under-samples the majority class to obtain a balanced set. A
perfectly balanced training set was obtained by generating 5 new cases for
each of the 45 observations with e-commerce (270 cases in total), and randomly
selecting 270 out of 275 cases without e-commerce. This way, the final training
set included 540 cases. Regarding the test set, it included the remaining 25%
of the initial observations (i.e., 106 websites), which were unequally distributed
among both classes (15 websites with e-commerce vs. 91 websites without).

Once the two data sets are prepared, the SAME production module is
trained following the procedure detailed above. Accordingly, the λ associated to the coefficient penalization parameter of the LASSO was estimated
by means of a 10-fold cross-validation procedure, whose results are shown in
Figure 4.2. By applying the LASSO, a binomial logistic regression with 60
predictors (equivalent to a $\ln(\lambda)$ value of -4.837, where the value of (λ) corresponds to the largest possible such that the cross-validation error is within
one standard error of the minimum) was selected out of the more than 150
raw features generated by the analysis module, as indicated by the dotted line
in Figure 4.2. Among the selected features, we found the private area and a
large number of keywords.

After training the production module, the model performance was evaluated by means of the test set. Table 4.2 shows the results in form of a confusion
matrix. As one can observe, the classification accuracy reached 90.6% on the

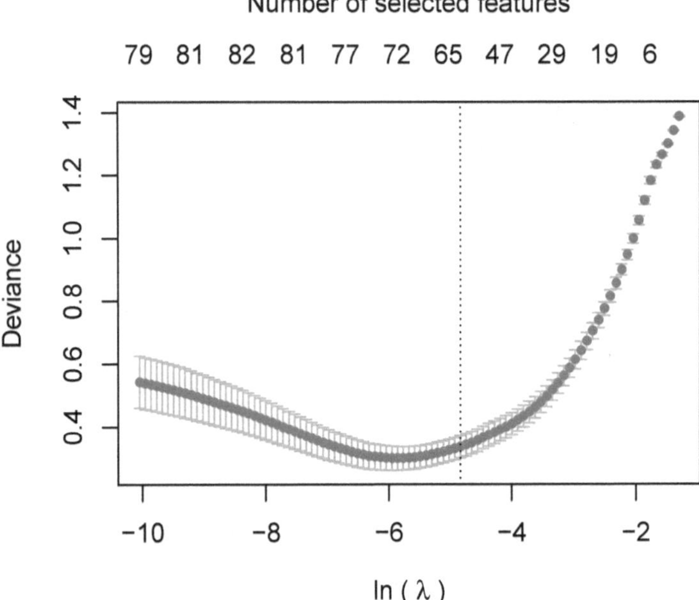

Figure 4.2: Cross-validation train error (with 5% confidence intervals) for a range of λ parameter values of the LASSO method for computing the automatic e-commerce indicator. The vertical dotted line indicates the value of λ in which the error is no more than one standard error above of the minimum, following the "one standard error rule"

test set, which is considerably high. After running the experiment 100 times with different train and test sets, the 95% confidence interval for the model's accuracy ranged from 83% to 93.4%.

The proportion of false positives and negatives among the misclassified cases is similar. False positives correspond to websites classified as having e-commerce that actually do not have this functionality, while false negatives correspond to websites whose e-commerce functionality was not detected by SAME. In the next section, a more detailed analysis of these cases is provided.

Table 4.2: Confusion matrix for the test set

		Real e-commerce availability	
		0	**1**
Predicted e-commerce availability	**0**	80.19%	3.77%
	1	5.66%	10.38%

To give a wider view of the performance of SAME, Figure 4.3 shows the ROC curve for the predictions on the test set. As one can observe, the model line (solid) is far from the diagonal that would represent a random model. The area under the curve (AUC) also evidences the discriminant power of the model; with a value of 0.9132 and a 95% confidence interval that ranges from 0.8333 to 0.9597, it is largely above the threshold of 0.7 for being considered very discriminant (Swets, 1988).

The performance of the LASSO was compared against other classifiers in order to check if, as hypothesized, it was the best for the case of this study. Results confirm that the LASSO achieve higher values for all metrics considered (see Appendix).

4.4.2.3 More insights on the model performance

Finally, to provide more insights on how the classification model works, the predicted probabilities are calculated for the original sample of 426 corporate websites and represented against some of their features. This way, it is easy to check that as hypothesized, a greater number of features and keywords is related to a greater probability of having e-commerce. This also permits to identify which cases are outliers in order to analyze them individually and obtain information that could help to improve the performance of SAME in the future.

Figure 4.4 shows the relationship between the probabilities calculated by the production module and the number of assembled features reflected in Table

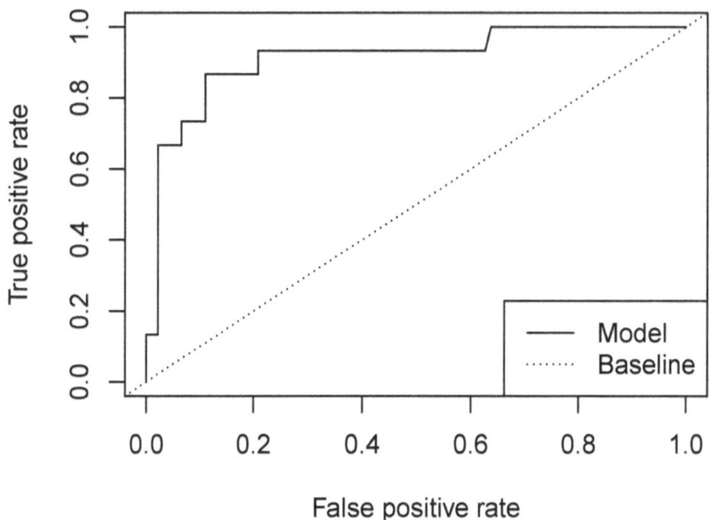

Figure 4.3: ROC curve corresponding to the test set

4.1 that are present in each website. The majority of websites with e-commerce have been assigned a probability greater than 0.5, so they are properly classified. In addition, it can be observed that most of these websites include a great number of the features, which is in line to what we expected in the research. The association of high probabilities with a large number of features makes that these cases are mainly located on the top right side of the plot. A more detailed analysis on the false negatives, which correspond to websites that offer e-commerce but are located near to the left side of Figure 4.4, revealed that most of them are caused by an incomplete crawling of the site by the capture module. This usually happens when parts of the website are

developed with Flash or *javascript* technologies, given that HTTrack provides
a limited support to them.

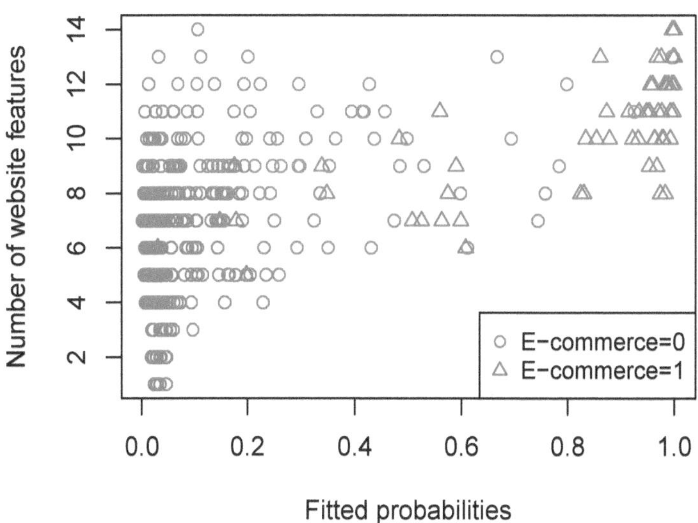

Figure 4.4: Relationship between the fitted probabilities of the production
module and the number of features available per website

About the websites without e-commerce, most of them have been assigned
a probability lower than 0.5, so they are classified as negative cases. This con-
firms that the model is identifying these cases properly, although the range in
the number of features detected on the websites is wider in this case. Notwithstanding this, it can also be appreciated that they are mainly located on
the bottom left side of the figure, which is what we expected. A more profound analysis on the false positives, which correspond to websites without
e-commerce that are located near to the right side of Figure 4.4, revealed

that, although evidences about the presence of e-commerce were found on the websites, the e-commerce functionality was available in a different URL with respect to the one analyzed, therefore it was manually coded as not offering e-commerce following the criteria employed in this study. Additionally, in some cases a variety of keywords selected as predictors by the LASSO are found on these sites, which means that these terms can be used in different contexts and are making reference to an activity which is not e-commerce.

Figure 4.5 shows the relationship between the probabilities calculated by the production module and the number of keyword matches (either HTML or href keywords) per website. The results of the model in this case are similar to those observed in Figure 4.4. Most of the websites with e-commerce are located on the right side of the graphic. As the cut point considered is 0.5, this indicates that they have been assigned probabilities greater than 0.5 by the model and so have been well predicted. The bulk of cases is concentrated among 10 and 40 keywords, meaning that the presence of e-commerce can be detected by a number of keywords.

Regarding the cases without e-commerce, most of them are located on the bottom left side of the plot. On the one hand, this indicates that they have been assigned probabilities lower than 0.5, thus being correctly classified. On the other hand, it indicates that these keywords are usually absent when the website do not have e-commerce, although some of them could appear (typically including between 0 and 20 keywords).

A detailed analysis of the misclassified cases point out some ideas on how to improve the system. False negatives due to an incomplete crawling suggest that these cases could be reduced by better dealing with sites that use *javascript* and Flash intensively. Other lines to explore how to improve performance include considering other HTML elements potentially related to e-commerce, or extending the selection of keywords to consider other words commonly used in e-commerce websites.

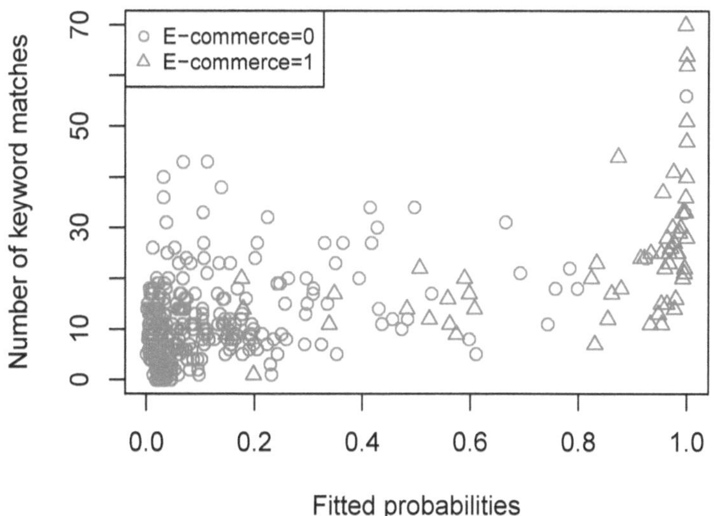

Figure 4.5: Relationship between the fitted probabilities of the production
module and the number of keywords (HTML and Href) available per website

4.5 Conclusions

The current digital environment in which the Internet provide us with fresh
data in abundance offers the chance to interpret and give value to all this
information in real time. To this end, Big Data analysis has emerged as a
particularly useful tool that could allow companies and governments to real-
time monitoring key aspects of the economy and thus implement more effective
strategies.

Focusing on the growing importance of e-commerce, this paper has proposed and developed SAME, which is an intelligent system to automatically

retrieve and analyze data from corporate websites to discover the adoption of e-commerce. Our proposal relies on a classification model that monitors e-commerce adoption in manufacturing firms by simply considering a selection of features from their websites. To do so, techniques such as web content mining and learning methods for Big Data were employed.

SAME has been tested and evaluated with the information retrieved from 426 corporate websites of firms located in France and Spain. After extracting the most relevant features from them and training the production module, the evaluation of the proposed system evidenced its accuracy for classifying firms into those that adopted e-commerce and those that did not (90.6% classification accuracy).

Detecting the presence of e-commerce on corporate websites from the automatic analysis of online data opens a new way for real-time and inexpensive monitoring. This implies a number of advantages in comparison to traditional monitoring methods based in surveys.

First, given its automatic nature, it opens up the opportunity to monitor e-commerce adoption at a large scale, thus obtaining highly granular information that otherwise would have required every firm to complete a survey. For the same reason, SAME makes it possible to track the evolution of this activity in real time. Thus, it is capable of providing us with more frequent information related to e-commerce than official surveys, which are usually conducted and processed annually.

In this way, government and institutions could make informed decisions earlier and, for instance, assess the impact of programs to promote digital sales in the short term, disaggregated by geographic area and economic sector. Moreover, business managers could also take advantage of the fresh information about e-commerce adoption in their activity sector in order to anticipate changes and reorient the strategies of companies.

Second, it constitutes a good complement to surveys. Since the information about e-commerce adoption can be discovered directly from the Web, without specifically asking firms, this frees some space in the questionnaire to include more complex matters that necessarily involve personal intervention.

Third, SAME provide researchers with a new source of information that could be very valuable when combined with other sources. For instance, when analyzing the factors which lie behind the adoption of e-commerce; or to focus a research only in the group of adopters.

As future work, we plan to improve SAME to increase the level of detail on the provided output. That is, to generate not only an indicator for e-commerce adoption, but also to give details on its implementation, such as the integration with other information systems of the company (e.g., ERP) or the connection with a payment gateway, as well as to determine which features contribute to this implementation being successful.

In this way, SAME could provide us with information about the degree in which the e-commerce is being used by the firms, to which extent it is included in the company strategies, and how to successfully implement it.

Appendix

Table 4.3: Comparison of classifiers performance

Metric	LASSO Logistic Regression	Classification Tree	Random Forests	SVM
Accuracy	0.9057	0.8585	0.8491	0.8679
Sensitivity	0.9341	0.8901	0.8791	0.9011
Specificity	0.7333	0.6667	0.6667	0.6667
AUC	0.9132	0.7520	0.7833	0.7719

Table 4.3 reflects the performance of four different classifiers: The LASSO logistic regression, which is the classifier used to develop the study; a Classification Tree; Random Forests; and a Support Vector Machine (SVM). It includes results regarding the metrics of accuracy, sensitivity, specificity and AUC, which are the most common for comparing how well a classifier perform.

Chapter 5

Do corporate websites' changes reflect firms' survival?

Chapter 5 is an adapted version of this published research paper:

- Title: Do corporate websites' changes reflect firms' survival?
- Authors: Desamparados Blazquez, Josep Domenech and Ana Debón
- Year of publication: 2018
- Journal: Online Information Review
- Volume: 42(6)
- Pages: 956-970
- DOI: 10.1108/OIR-11-2016-0321

5.1 Introduction

Business demography is one of the economic aspects that attracts more attention from governments and policy makers. Indeed most official statistics
institutions (e.g., Eurostat, Office for National Statistics of Spain, Australian
Bureau of Statistics) carry out detailed surveys to monitor the active population of firms, their birth, survival and death. The interest shown in busi-ness
demography statistics relies on the important role they play in economic
growth, productivity and employment (Eurostat and OECD, 2007).

In the Digital Era, the prominent role of the Internet in economy and
society, along with the development of advanced computer systems and archi-

tectures, opens up new ways of monitoring economic activities (Blazquez and Domenech, 2014; Vaughan, 2014) and, therefore, business demography. The Internet and the World Wide Web (WWW) have become basic tools for the daily activities of individuals and companies, whose importance is increasing in both developed and developing countries. For consumers, the WWW is a convenient instrument to find information on products and services, and if available, to purchase them online. For companies, the WWW is an inexpensive channel to not only offer information about their products, services and activities, but to also make transactions with customers more quickly and more flexibly. In this context, companies have massively developed their websites in order to be present on the digital channels. For instance, 75% of companies are present on the WWW in Spain (INE, 2016), which is the country on which our empirical analysis focuses.

Corporate websites constitute the most formal and official representation of firms on the Internet. Generally, firms describe their main activities, products and intended strategies on their websites. Therefore, corporate website contents are necessarily connected to business activity to some extent, which has been recently studied from different perspectives. For instance, evidence has been found for the relation of website contents to technology adoption (Youtie et al., 2012; Arora et al., 2013), innovation activities (Arora et al., 2016; Gök et al., 2015), firms' growth (Li et al., 2016), and firms' export orientation (Blazquez and Domenech, 2014, 2018b).

Once it has been proved that firms' activities emerge on their corporate website, the question as to whether firms' inactivity is also manifested on their website arises. Keeping a website online involves some costs, such as fees for domain name registrations or server hosting upkeep. Furthermore, costs increase when companies wish to keep website contents and related technologies up to date. Active companies are expected to regularly modify their website to include new products or services, renew its design and offer additional functionalities, or to inform potential customers about new offers or promotions. Since keeping the website updated requires firms to mobilize some resources (financial, working or both), it is plausible that only active and healthy firms would invest their resources to that end. Therefore if a company dies, this event is likely to be manifested on its website as lacking updates or simply as being down.

Most academic research conducted on firms' survival has focused on the factors that contribute to keep companies alive. The firm's age, size, productivity or profitability have been widely studied as determinant factors that contribute to firms' survival. Despite the important role that the WWW plays in today's business, there are no studies relating the WWW to firms' survival. Corporate websites are a fresh source of business information as they are publicly accessible and provide access to high granularity (company level) data which are generally updated regularly. For these reasons, they have been used to analyze some company behaviors or strategies. Nevertheless, the approach of employing corporate websites to analyze firms' survival is novel.

This paper analyzes to what extent changes in corporate websites reflect firms' survival. This work hypothesizes that if a firm dies, it is very likely that its website goes down, which could happen shortly before or after the firm's death. If this relationship exists, then the corporate website status (down, unchanged or updated), whose retrieval and tracking are inexpensive, could help monitor firms' survival. To evaluate our proposal, the corporate website changes and firm activity status of a panel of Spanish firms were monitored for 7 years and analyzed. Multi-period logistic regressions and survival analysis were run to infer the firms' activity status. The results showed that the corporate website status clearly reflects the firm's status.

The rest of the paper is organized as follows. Next section reviews the literature on firms' survival and the detection of economic information through web analysis. The subsequent section describes the data used and the methodology applied for the empirical analysis. The following section describes the results, including a data overview and a comprehensive analysis of model estimations. Finally, the last section draws some concluding remarks.

5.2 Theoretical background

This section provides background on firms' survival analysis and the detection of economic activities on the WWW. First, the related literature on firms' survival analysis is reviewed, reporting the firm-related variables which researchers have paid more attention to. Second, a review on the detection of firms' activities through web and online data is provided, motivating the exploration of whether firms' inactivity could also be detected through their websites.

5.2.1 Firms' survival analysis

Firms' survival is a hot topic for researchers because of its implications for business success, economic stability and growth. However, it was not until the 1990s, promoted by the increasing economic globalization, when the academic community started to focus on analyzing firms' survival. Firms started to face new challenges in a more complex and turbulent environment, which is the reason why determining which characteristics or actions could help them survive was more necessary than ever before.

The seminal work of Evans (1987), and other later ones like Audretsch (1991), Mata and Portugal (1994) and Geroski (1995), helped expand the field of firms' survival, focusing on a systematic analysis of which industry-specific and firm-specific factors affected companies' survival, and in which direction.

Regarding firm-related structural variables, firm size and age have been widely explored since they have been considered stylized facts related to firm survival (Geroski, 1995). Generally, firm size has been found to increase the likelihood of a firm's survival, especially for new entrants (Agarwal and Audretsch, 2001; Cefis and Marsili, 2005; Geroski et al., 2010). Larger firms usually have more financial and human resources available as well as a solid structure after reaching a certain production level. These factors could help reduce the risk of mortality.

A similar pattern has been exhibited by firm age, which has been found to principally increase the likelihood of survival (Audretsch et al., 2000; Manjón-

Antolín and Arauzo-Carod, 2008). Older firms have had the possibility of acquiring experience in how the market works and which strategies are more profitable for them. This could help them survive compared to newcomers. That is, the effect of experience on firms' survival is generally positive.

Other structural variables whose relationship with firms' survival has been consistently studied by researchers include the firm's debt structure, its level of productivity and its level of profitability (Audretsch et al., 2000; Delmar et al., 2013; Görg and Spaliara, 2014). These variables are closely related to the firm's level of success, stability and health, and are thus potentially influential for the likelihood of a firm to survive.

The technological intensity of the activity sector in which the company operates has also been considered in other firms' survival studies (Esteve-Pérez and Mañez-Castillejo, 2008; Giovannetti et al., 2011). The first findings pointed out that firms had more difficulties to survive in high-technological sectors. However, an opposite pattern was found later; providing highly technological products and services requires firms to develop sophisticated skills, to focus on innovation and knowledge, and these factors are potential contributors to firms' survival particularly within today's complex economic frame.

More recent studies continue providing insights into how the classical firm structural factors, e.g., size, age or financial ratios, and environmental factors like financial crises, location or the specific business life cycle, contribute to increase or decrease the likelihood of firms' survival (Basile et al., In Press; Gémar et al., 2016; Guariglia et al., 2016). The results of most reviewed literature works aim to serve mainly as guidelines in managers' decision-making processes, who could use this information to run or promote strategies that can contribute to firms' survival.

However, none of the studies in the literature has analyzed the relationship between firms' survival and corporate websites. The role of corporate websites in the firms' strategies is basic in today's digital society, and is expected to gain importance in the future. While accounting data have been useful for predicting firm's failure, they are not perfect measures of a firm's operational and financial status (Astebro and Winter, 2012), so complementing them with online data could offer a better idea of a firm's health.

For these reasons, it is relevant to confirm to what extent the corporate website status is related to the firm's status of activity, and to explore if the information provided on the website can be used for monitoring a firm's survival. The next section reviews the literature on the suitability of the WWW to reflect business activity, which motivated our study on checking whether it also reflects a firm's inactivity, i.e. a firm's death.

5.2.2 Capturing firms' economic activities through web data

Every minute of the day, thousands of individuals, companies and public bodies generate, post and share information through the internet. These online activities leave a digital footprint behind that can be tracked and, if properly processed and analyzed, can help describe their economic and social behavior.

The detection of behavioral and consumer patterns, and economic and business activities, through online data is an incipient research field whose importance is starting to increase at the same time as the adoption of the Internet is expanding worldwide. This generalized expansion in Internet use is affecting the way companies do business, which are being enforced by the current digital context to go online. To do so, firms generally start by implementing websites, which are the most official representation of their image and could, at the same time, be used as a commercial channel.

Indeed websites are relevant sources of online data whose potential for detecting and monitoring economic activities has remained unexplored until quite recently. Websites have a complex structure that differs from one case to another, making the process of extracting, processing and analyzing information difficult to standardize and automate to allow massive data exploitation compared to traditional databases. However, websites also present many advantages, such as: they are publicly accessible, provide fresh information and can be analyzed at any time, which traditional databases generally do not. In particular, corporate websites are attracting more attention because they are

being increasingly adopted by firms, which normally use them to reflect their
characteristics, products and intended strategies. Therefore, websites have
become rich sources of business information. For these reasons, specific technologies and methodologies for extracting and analyzing web data are being
developed (Munzert et al., 2015).

The first works about detecting economic or business information on corporate websites were published a decade ago. Following a non-automated
approach, Overbeeke and Snizek (2005) captured different corporate culture
dimensions by analyzing the text and images available on a set of corporate
websites, while Meroño-Cerdan and Soto-Acosta (2007) found that external
web content related positively to firm performance.

Firms' corporate social responsibility and sustainability strategies, and
their levels of adoption, have also been successfully detected in corporate websites contents (Gallego Álvarez et al., 2008; Tagesson et al., 2009; Tang et al.,
2015). This has been done, for instance, by detecting the occurrence number
of keywords related to green products (Albino et al., 2009). This measure
has been extended and successfully used in other studies that have focused
on novel technology industries. In their work, Libaers et al. (2010) found six
types of business models for commercializing novel technology by automatically analyzing the frequency with which specific keywords were present on
the corporate websites of the firms under study.

Following an automatic approach, Youtie et al. (2012) and Arora et al.
(2013) applied web scraping and content analysis techniques to corporate
websites, including the count of keywords, in order to track the technology
adoption strategies of firms on emerging technology sectors. Innovation is
another relevant topic which has been recently detected through web mining techniques. Gök et al. (2015) and Arora et al. (2016) successfully detected
firms' R&D activities by analyzing corporate websites contents. For their part,
Li et al. (2016) tracked firms' sales growth in a Triple Helix context.

The first attempt to generalize the automatic analysis of corporate websites to discover economic information was introduced by Domenech et al.
(2012). This work presents a web data mining system architecture that man-

ages the process of crawling and analyzing corporate websites, which was successfully tested for finding web-based indicators for firms' size. This system was adapted by Blazquez and Domenech (2018b) to detect firms' export orientation by automatically analyzing their corporate websites since a previous manual analysis found that websites potentially reflect such business activity (Blazquez and Domenech, 2014).

Based on previous research, in which corporate websites were demonstrated to reflect economic information and business activities, this paper hypothesizes that detecting firms' inactivity by analyzing the data retrieved from corporate websites is also possible.

5.3 Data and methodology

This section first describes the structure of the data used herein and how it was obtained. Second, it reviews the methodology employed, which relies on multi-period logistic regression models to detect the ability of website status to predict firm's activity status, and a duration model to provide a deeper understanding of how the web status relates to a firm's survival.

5.3.1 Data

The initial study sample included 780 companies[1] established in Spain from manufacturing, services and other sectors (NACE Rev.2[2] codes 10-95), all of which were active and had a website in 2008. The sample was retrieved by a simple random sampling design from the SABI database (Bureau van Dijk, 2010), being eligible all firms in the database that met four criteria: being active, being located in Spain, belonging to any of the mentioned activity sectors, and having a website; all of them referred to year 2008, in which this study begins. The data set consists of a panel of economic and online

---

[1]From the total sample of 780 firms, 92% were small and medium-sized (SMEs), in line with the prevailing productive structure in Spain (DGIPYME, 2017).

[2]Statistical Classification of Economic Activities in the European Community (Eurostat, 2008)

data for these firms for years 2008 to 2014. The economic information was
retrieved from company financial records by accessing a more recent version
of the SABI database in January 2016, and 2014 was the last year for which
complete company economic records were found.

The online information was collected by accessing the corporate websites
with the Wayback Machine of the Internet Archive (Kahle and Gilliat, 2016),
which is a public and free repository of snapshots of about 484 billion web
pages. The Internet Archive captures and stores websites on a daily basis,
allowing users to access them and track their history and evolution over time.
However, there are some limitations as to its use: its inability to capture
websites that prevented themselves from being explored by web crawlers by
means of the robots exclusion standard (i.e. robots.txt); its limited ability
to capture Flash content; the fact that it does not crawl the whole WWW,
so some websites are not captured and, therefore, their evolution over time
cannot be tracked; and that not every website is frequently captured, even
some of them less than once a year. These limitations prevented us from
tracking the evolution of some corporate websites.

For these reasons, the firms whose websites were not found in the Wayback
Machine were removed from the initial sample. This gave a final sample of
720 companies to be included in the study, of which 674 survived the whole
time period, while the remaining 46 died at some time. Only the years from
2010 to 2014 were included in the data analysis presented below in order to
track any website changes compared to the previous year and to align the
website status to the time at which financial information is available. In order
to take into account the different moments of time at which company data are
available, information from the financial statements was lagged two periods in
the empirical analyses. That is, it is possible to know the corporate website
status at time t, but at this time the most recent financial statements available
correspond to $t - 2$.

Some website captures in a particular year t of the study period were not
available in the Wayback Machine. This resulted in an unbalanced panel with

3254 observations, of which 3152 corresponded to the firms that survived to 2014, and the remaining 102 to those that died during the study period.

To account for changes in the corporate websites, the procedure followed consisted in querying the Wayback Machine with the URL of each company's website and checking the homepage for each year studied. The observed changes were coded into the variable *Web_status*, which could take five different values depending on the status or type of change experimented each year. These five levels are defined as:

- **Code 1**: the website is down. This includes the websites that do not work (e.g., HTTP Error 404 Not Found) or whose domain name has expired or is for sale.

- **Code 2**: the website remains unchanged. This includes the cases in which the website remains exactly the same as its previous year's version.

- **Code 3**: the website has undergone minor changes. These changes include the removal or addition of sections, options, pictures and contents.

- **Code 4**: the website has undergone major changes. These changes refer to a new website design, so that it completely differs from to the previous year's version; this may imply a change in the technology used to build the website.

- **Code 5**: the website has not been captured by the Wayback Machine. These cases were processed as missing data and were removed from the final sample as it was impossible to determine the website status.

The data set also included the economic variables classically related to firms' survival according to the reviewed literature. These variables, together with the firm's status (active or inactive), were retrieved from the SABI database and complemented with the information taken from the Official Gazette of the Commercial Registry[3] to account for merges and acquisitions. The following economic variables were retrieved:

---

[3]BORME, from their initials in Spanish, 'Boletín Oficial del Registro Mercantil'.

- $Active_{i,t}$: Dichotomous variable that takes a value of 1 if firm i is active in year t, and 0 otherwise[4].

- $Size_{i,t}$: Quantitative variable measured as the logarithm of the number of employees of firm i in year t. It is a proxy to firm size.

- $Age_{i,t}$: Quantitative variable measured as the number of years since firm i was established up to year t. It is a proxy to the firm's experience.

- $Debt_{i,t}$: Quantitative variable measured as the percentage of debt of firm i in year t.

- $Productivity_{i,t}$: Quantitative variable measured as the value added per employee (in millions of euros) of firm i in year t.

- $Profitability_{i,t}$: Quantitative variable measured as the ratio of economic profitability of firm i in year t. This ratio, known as 'Return on Assets (ROA)', is obtained from dividing the operating profit by total assets.

- $High\_tech_{i,t}$: Dichotomous variable that takes a value of 1 when the economic activity of firm i in year t is considered of high or medium-high technological intensity according to the Eurostat Classification (Eurostat, 2014), and 0 otherwise.

5.3.2 Multi-period logistic regression

In a first approach, firms' survival was studied by multi-period logistic regression models. These models are useful for examining how some independent variables are related to a dependent variable when the data used as input include individuals observed over time, which was the case of the present study, and have been applied successfully in existing firms' survival studies (Bridges and Guariglia, 2008; Jacobson and von Schedvin, 2015).

---

[4]We considered inactive the following firm status: in extinction; in dissolution; in liquidation; in a finished receivership where dissolution or liquidation has been ordered, but is not yet done; or in receivership in progress (if it is the most recent status and no additional information is available), except when the firm had been taken over or had merged (Eurostat and OECD, 2007).

The dependent variable in this research is whether or not the firm's status is active ($Active_{i,t}$), which is a dichotomous variable that makes logistic regression suitable for analyzing the relation with covariates. The models used include fixed-time effects to account for the changing economic and politic situation that affects the baseline probability of being active each year. Analytically, the model is represented as:

$$\theta_{i,t} = \ln\left(\frac{P(y_{i,t}=1)}{1-P(y_{i,t}=1)}\right) = \beta' X_{i,t} + \gamma_t, \tag{5.1}$$

where $\theta_{i,t}$ is the logit, $P(y_{i,t}=1)$ is the probability of occurrence of status "1" of the dependent variable $y_{i,t}$, β' is the vector of regression coefficients, $X_{i,t}$ is the vector of covariates for firm i in year t, and γ_t are the time specific parameters that reflect the unobservable events that affect all firms each year.

This model is used to first assess the relation between the WWW and firms' status, as it estimates the probability of a firm being active given its website status in a first specification, and given this website status and a number of economic variables in a second specification. Both model specifications controlled for the economic juncture or period effect by including dummies for each year considered in the study. Accordingly, the first model was defined as follows:

$$\theta_{i,t} = \ln\left(\frac{P(Active_{i,t}=1)}{1-P(Active_{i,t}=1)}\right) = \beta_0 + \alpha Web\_status_{i,t} + \gamma_t, \tag{5.2}$$

where $P(Active_{i,t}=1)$ is the probability that firm i is active in year t, and the logit, $\theta_{i,t}$ is regressed on the explanatory variable $Web\_status_{i,t}$ and the fixed-effect of time, captured by γ_t.

An extended model was specified by including also the firms' economic variables that can affect firm survival according to the literature. The variables that were finally selected were those that varied with an admissible level of significance ($p<0.05$) between both groups of firms and did not highly correlate. This second specification was defined as follows:

$$\theta_{i,t} = \ln\left(\frac{P(Active_{i,t} = 1)}{1 - P(Active_{i,t} = 1)}\right) \tag{5.3}$$

$$= \beta_0 + \alpha Web\_status_{i,t} + \beta' Z_{i,t-2} + \rho High\_tech_{i,t-2} + \gamma_t,$$

where $P(Active_{i,t} = 1)$ is the probability that firm i is active in year t,
and the logit, $\theta_{i,t}$, is regressed on the variable based on corporate website,
$Web\_status_{i,t}$, the vector of economic quantitative variables $Z_{i,t-2}$ which includes $Size_{i,t-2}$, $Debt_{i,t-2}$, $Productivity_{i,t-2}$ and $Profitability_{i,t-2}$, the economic categorical variable $High\_tech_{i,t-2}$ and the fixed-effect of time, captured
by γ_t.

Having confirmed the relation between the WWW and firms' status with
both regressions, a duration model is applied to estimate the firm's probability
of surviving one time period or more given the corporate website status.

5.3.3 Survival analysis

The relation of the firm's website status with its duration, the latter defined as
the time elapsed (during the observed period) until a firm fails, was analyzed
through survival models (also known as duration models (Lancaster, 1990)).
These models are useful for predicting events like failures or deaths on a subject
(e.g. firm, machine, system, product or patient). Specifically, time and other
predictive variables are considered to estimate the hazard of failure or death
during a particular time period.

In survival analysis, the hazard function $h(t)$ is the one used for conducting
regressions. In this study, the hazard function was estimated through a cloglog
generalized linear model, which is the equivalent to the discrete time version of
the Cox proportional hazards model (Jenkins, 1995). It has been successfully
applied in previous firms' survival studies for data collected on an annual basis
(Tsoukas, 2011; Görg and Spaliara, 2014; Guariglia et al., 2016), which is this
case. The proportional hazard model assumes that the hazard rate depends
only on the time at risk, $h_0(t)$ (the baseline hazard) and on the vector of

explanatory variables, X. This is the rate at which firms die in year t, provided they survived the previous year, $t - 1$. It is expressed as:

$$h(t, X) = h_0(t) \, \exp(\beta' X) \qquad (5.4)$$

Particularly, the discrete-time hazard function (with period-specific effects) takes the following specification:

$$h(t, X) = 1 - \exp[-\exp(\beta' X + \gamma_t)], \qquad (5.5)$$

where β' is the regression coefficient vector that describes how the hazard varies in response to explanatory vector X of the covariates, and γ_t captures the period-specific effects on the hazard.

For this study, this duration model was specified as follows:

$$h(t, Web\_status) = 1 - \exp[-\exp(\beta_0 + \alpha Web\_status + \gamma_t)], \qquad (5.6)$$

where $h(t, Web\_status)$ is the hazard rate; that is, the rate at which firms become inactive at time t provided they were active in year $t - 1$, which is modeled through the explanatory variable Web_status and the period-specific effect, γ_t.

5.4 Results

This section first shows some descriptive statistics and group comparisons to provide a data overview. Second, two multi-period logistic regressions are built and compared to evaluate to what extent the Web_status variable captures the company's activity status. Finally, these results are complemented with a duration model.

5.4.1 Descriptive statistics and group comparisons

The descriptive statistics of the whole data set are reported in Table 5.1. As we can see, the sample is dominated by active firms (96.9% of the sample) which operate in a low-technology sector (81%) and that have a moderate level of debt (61%). This table evidences the absence of high correlations among variables, which means that there was no high risk of information redundancy and multicollinearity when estimating the regression models.

Table 5.1: Global descriptive statistics and correlation matrix

Variable	Mean	SD	1	2	3	4	5	6	7
1. *Active*	0.969	0.174							
2. *Web_status*	2.618	0.868	0.272						
3. *Size*	3.855	1.241	0.046	0.149					
4. *Age*	24.823	14.318	0.007	0.022	0.258				
5. *Debt*	60.470	31.608	−0.127	−0.009	0.016	−0.140			
6. *Productivity*	0.270	4.071	0.007	0.021	−0.129	−0.042	0.046		
7. *Profitability*	1.099	22.526	0.112	0.046	−0.005	0.005	−0.291	0.044	
8. *High_tech*	0.199	0.399	0.076	0.143	0.207	−0.062	−0.048	−0.021	−0.005

Procedures employed: Pearson's r coefficient for pairs of continuous variables; Point-biserial coefficient for pairs of a continuous and a binary variable; Phi coefficient for pairs of binary variables; and Eta for pairs of a continuous and a categorical variable with more than two levels. (Cohen et al., 2002)

The first column of Table 5.2 summarizes the behavior of corporate websites by showing the distribution of the *Web_status* variable across the sample. It indicates that most websites remained unchanged (37.7%) or underwent a moderate change (36.4%) compared with the previous year. Only 8.8% of the observations presented a down website, while 17.1% of them had totally changed. To illustrate the association with the other variables, the numeric value of *Web_status* is also included in Table 5.1.

In order to test whether the variables behaved differently depending on the firm's status (active or inactive), statistical techniques of group differences were employed. Pearson's Chi-squared test was applied to the categorical variables, whose results are reported in Table 5.2. Statistically significant differences were found for the technological intensity, being active firms more associated with technology-intensive sectors than those that became inactive (20.5% vs. 2.9%). For the website status, statistically significant differences were found between active and inactive firms. For the latter, most

Table 5.2: Descriptive statistics of qualitative variables and group comparisons

	All (N=3254)	*Active*(0) (N=102)	*Active*(1) (N=3152)	Chi-squared (*p*-value)
Active(0)	3.1%			
Active(1)	96.9%			
High_tech(0)	80.1%	97.1%	79.5%	
High_tech(1)	19.9%	2.9%	20.5%	0.000
Web_status(1)	8.8%	50.0%	7.5%	
Web_status(2)	37.7%	40.2%	37.6%	
Web_status(3)	36.4%	7.8%	37.3%	
Web_status(4)	17.1%	2.0%	17.6%	0.000

Notes: *Web_status*(1): Down; *Web_status*(2): Unchanged; *Web_status*(3): Minor change; *Web_status*(4): Major change.

websites were down (50%) or remained unchanged (40.2%), while minor or major changes were found only in the remaining 9.8%.

In contrast, content changes were found in more than half of the active firms' websites, mainly minor changes (37.3%). This was expected because website design forms part of the firm's corporate image, which is not renewed yearly by most companies. Instead, minor changes to keep information up-to-date are frequently made by active firms. Moreover, down websites are not common among active companies (7.5%). The presence of unchanged websites (37.6%) was similar to the case of inactive firms, so this website status is not as indicative of the firm's status as the cases in which changes were made.

With the quantitative variables, normality and homogeneity of variance were checked both graphically and numerically. As none of the variables fulfilled both assumptions, the non-parametric Mann-Whitney U test was employed, which is based on the median (Anderson et al., 2014). These results are reflected in Table 5.3. Most economic variables showed statistically different values for the active firms compared to the firms that had died during the observed period. The log number of employees was statistically higher for

the active firms (3.761 vs. 3.401), so firm size relates to the firm's duration to
some extent.

Table 5.3: Descriptive statistics of quantitative variables and group comparisons

	$Active(0)$ (N=102)	$Active(1)$ (N=3152)	Mann-Whitney U (p-value)
$Size$	3.761	3.401	0.007
Age	21.501	22.815	0.875
$Debt$	88.990	60.810	0.000
$Productivity$	30.947	48.787	0.000
$Profitability$	-3.775	2.000	0.000

About the firm's age, no statistically significant differences were found, so
firms seem to die with the same probability regardless of their age. The debt
value was much higher for inactive firms (88.99% vs. 60.81%), which is indicative of the detrimental effect that high levels of debt have on firms' health,
and thus on their continuity. Active firms were associated with statistically
higher levels of productivity and profitability than inactive ones. High productivity levels are connected to overall better firm performance, which would
contribute to having a higher profitability. Both these measures are related to
the company's health so as expected, healthier companies continue with their
activities more frequently.

5.4.2 Multi-period logistic regression models

In this section, we shed light on the role played by corporate websites status
on firms' probability of being active. First, a multi-period logistic regression
model based on the Web_status variable was built, as specified in Equation
(5.2).

Table 5.4 provides the estimation results for this model, including the estimated regression coefficients (β), Odds Ratios (OR), Standard Errors (SE),

z-values and p-values. The OR is a measure of the association between the different website statuses and the firm's status, and is calculated as the exponent of the coefficients. Thus, an OR over 1 indicates that the probability that a firm is active increases with a given independent variable (in this case, each particular website status). If it is lower than 1, it indicates that this probability decreases, while if it equals 1 then there is no association between the independent and dependent variable.

Table 5.4: Multi-period logistic regression with web status. Dependent variable: *Active*

Variables	β	OR	SE	z-value	p-value
(Intercept)	3.483	32.557	0.598	5.827	0.000
$Web\_status(2)$	1.628	5.094	0.227	7.158	0.000
$Web\_status(3)$	3.423	30.661	0.390	8.786	0.000
$Web\_status(4)$	3.970	52.985	0.727	5.460	0.000
Observations	3,254				
Log-likelihood	-349.349				

Notes: $Web\_status(2)$: Unchanged; $Web\_status(3)$: Minor change; $Web\_status(4)$: Major change. Time dummies were included.

For this web-based model, the results show that the observed web statuses have a statistically significant effect on the probability of a company being active. As website activity increases, the probability of a firm being active also increases. The estimate that corresponds to the website status 'Unchanged' (Code 2) is positive, which means that having a working website, even if its contents or look are not changed compared to the previous year, increases the probability of a firm being active with respect to having a down website (Code 1, which was taken as the baseline level). Indeed, the probability of a firm with an unchanged website being active is 5 times (or 409.4% higher) than that of a firm whose website is down, as indicated by the OR.

Updating websites to a minor (Code 3) or major (Code 4) extent increases the probability of a firm being active, as expected. Furthermore, the increase found is dramatically high in both cases. The probability of a firm being active when it moderately changes its website is 30-fold higher compared to a firm whose website is down, while it is more than 50-fold higher when a website has been completely renewed. These results are in line with what was hypothesized: healthy firms invest more in maintaining and updating their websites. Hence, the more activity they evidence on their website, the more likely they are active. It is noteworthy that this does not mean that updating websites helps firms remain active, but it strongly reflects firm's active status.

Once the relationship between the corporate websites' status and the firms' status was evidenced, the extended specification given by Equation (5.3) was estimated. It included the website status variable and the structural variables selected for their potential relation to firms' survival, and for the significant variation across active and inactive firms.

As reported in Table 5.5, the effect of each website status on the probability of being active remains positive, and statistically significant and high. Regarding the economic variables, only the firm's debt structure shows a statistically significant effect. Its negative coefficient indicates that as the amount of a firm's debt increases, its probability of being active decreases. Indeed, it decreases by 1.8% for each percentage point increase in debt.

Although the remaining economic variables showed differences in the univariate level, they do not help explain the firm's status at the multivariate level. On the one hand, such economic variables are related to a firm's status, but only to a limited extent as a large number of other factors, such as the firm's strategic decisions or specific market situations, can contribute to the death of firms with a wide range of characteristics (small or large, more or less productive, from any activity sector, etc.). On the other hand, website status has been revealed to be a clear indicator of a firm's status. So these economic variables were unable to complement the information displayed on the web.

Given that the relationship between corporate website status and firms' status was demonstrated, the next section went a step further to complement this analysis and to confer the study a different point of view. To do so, a survival analysis was conducted.

Table 5.5: Multi-period logistic regression with web and structural variables. Dependent variable: *Active*

Variables	β	OR	SE	z-value	p-value
(Intercept)	3.917	50.249	0.974	4.023	0.000
$Web\_status(2)$	1.579	4.850	0.395	4.001	0.000
$Web\_status(3)$	2.490	12.061	0.522	4.768	0.000
$Web\_status(4)$	3.242	25.585	0.951	3.410	0.001
$Size$	0.206	1.229	0.169	1.218	0.223
$Debt$	−0.018	0.982	0.006	−3.053	0.002
$Productivity$	0.034	0.193	1.034	0.283	0.777
$Profitability$	0.005	1.005	0.011	0.443	0.658
$High\_tech$	10.811	49,563.01	960.4	0.019	0.985
Observations	3,034				
Log-likelihood	−154.116				

Notes: $Web\_status(2)$: Unchanged; $Web\_status(3)$: Minor change; $Web\_status(4)$: Major change. Time dummies were included.

5.4.3 Survival analysis

This section describes the survival analysis conducted for modeling the hazard of a firm's death at certain times depending on website status. Since the data in this study were collected on an annual basis, a time-discrete duration model was built, as specified in Equation (5.6).

Table 5.6 offers the estimation results for this model, including the estimated regression coefficients (β), Hazard Ratios (HR), Standard Errors (SE), z-values and p-values. The HR, calculated as the exponent of coefficients, are a measure of how often an event happens in one group compared to how often it happens in another group over time. In this case, they measure how often the different website statuses happen in the groups of active and inactive firms. Thus an HR above 1 indicates that the hazard of death increases with the corresponding website status. If it is lower than 1, it means that this hazard decreases, while if it equals 1 then there is no difference in survival between the two groups being compared.

Table 5.6: Discrete-time duration model. Dependent variable: $1 - Active$

Variables	β	HR	SE	z-value	p-value
(Intercept)	-4.942	0.007	1.029	-4.802	0.000
$Web\_status(2)$	-1.202	0.301	0.348	-3.454	0.001
$Web\_status(3)$	-2.480	0.084	0.484	-5.128	0.000
$Web\_status(4)$	-2.764	0.063	0.753	-3.668	0.000
Observations	$3,194$				
Log-likelihood	-195.262				

Notes: $Web\_status(2)$: Unchanged; $Web\_status(3)$: Minor change; $Web\_status(4)$: Major change. Time dummies were included.

The negative and statistically significant coefficient estimates indicate that the firms whose websites are unchanged (Code 2), or undergo minor (Code 3) or major changes (Code 4) compared to the previous year, are exposed to a significantly lower hazard than the firms whose corporate websites are down (Code 1, which is the baseline web status). Specifically, the hazard ratio for the "Unchanged" website status (Code 2) indicates that the firms whose website contents are the same as the previous year have 0.301 times the hazard of death of the firms whose website is down; that is, their death hazard is 69.9% lower. The death hazard for firms which made minor changes in their websites (Code 3) is 91.6% lower than for those with down websites, while the percentage reaches 93.7% when the changes made are major (Code 4). As we can observe, the death hazard lowers at the same time as website activity increases. These results are consistent with those of the multi-period logistic regressions, and confirm the strong relationship between corporate website status and a firm's survival.

5.5 Conclusions

Business demography is a major area of interest for researchers and policy-makers because the creation and failure of companies have a huge impact on the production and employment in all the economies. In the current context, in which digital communications and Internet contents reflect society's main behavior, a new challenge arises: that of relating business demography with the WWW evolution.

This paper analyzed and confirmed the connection of a company's activity status to the corporate website's activity status. This was done by tracking corporate websites and statuses of firms for 7 years, and then analyzing their relation with logistic regressions and a survival model. Logistic regression estimates that major changes in the corporate website increase the odds of a firm being active by more than 50-fold compared to a down website. In terms of survival, corporate website changes are related to a predicted death hazard more than 90% lower. Since both methods gave similar results, this means that the corporate website is a robust indicator of a firm's activity status.

These results open up new possibilities to monitor business demography. Web data capture a firm's status, while access to corporate websites is open and inexpensive. This means that it is possible to build online indicators to nowcast and monitor business death rates. Unlike traditional official statistics methods, which rely on surveys done on a population sample that take time to be processed, monitoring the WWW could fast reach the entire population of companies with a website. This can be done in a very short period thanks to the digital nature of the WWW, which allows firms' information to be automatically retrieved and analyzed. This, in turn, allows policy-makers and other consumers of official statistics to obtain short-term estimates of the business demography, which would eventually turn into more informed decisions.

Among the limitations of this study, first, it is worth noting that only the homepage of the website was analyzed; that is, no changes in inner sections were taken into account. Second, the sample only includes companies based in Spain, so generalizing the results to different countries must be done cautiously. Finally, we must emphasize that we describe how website status correlates with a company's activity status, without causal analysis. Although this is useful for monitoring purposes, our results do not indicate that managers should continuously change corporate websites to increase company survival.

Chapter 6

Conclusions

6.1   Main contributions

In an era characterized by the daily generation of an unprecedented quantity of social and economic data on the WWW, along with the increasing need to take fast decisions by firms and policy-makers in a greater and greater competitive environment, the opportunity to take advantage of these data arises. The chance to obtain regular, accurate predictions about a variety of social and economic behaviors brings to light, at the same time, the necessity to deeply understand how to properly treat, store, process and analyze these new kind of data, web-based Big Data, in order to transform them into useful information for real-time monitoring and decision-making.

In this context, this book has focused on generating knowledge about the viability of producing economic indicators with data retrieved, processed and analyzed from corporate websites with web scraping and data analysis techniques. To do so, four specific objectives were proposed, as enumerated in the introductory chapter, all of which have been successfully achieved.

The starting objective of this book was to complete a literature review about the state of the art of the research field to which it belongs. This study field is the use of Big Data (and more particularly, online data) for producing economic (and social) indicators. A comprehensive literature review has been performed, from which four contributions have derived: the proposal of a taxonomy to classify the non-traditional sources of social and economic data (that include corporate websites, the principal source of data in this book); the proposal of a taxonomy to classify the non-traditional methods to structure, model and assess the performance of such data; the proposal of an integrative data lifecycle that includes all the stages needed for fully managing Big Data in a socio-economic context; and the design of a Big Data architecture to deal with the integration, analysis and governance of Big Data from a social and economic nature.

After establishing this framework, the rest of the work conducted in book has been focused on the design and evaluation of three economic indicators with data retrieved from corporate websites. We have applied a methodology developed on our own to design, evaluate and validate these economic web-based indicators. This methodology can be summarized into five main steps: first, we define a number of variables retrievable from websites, arguing their potential relation with the economic variable to be predicted; second, we access the corporate websites and manually codify the values of these variables; third, we automate the retrieval of these web variables by employing a web scraping system (that downloads the whole websites and then processes the variables we are interested in); fourth, we compare the manual and automatic web-based variables to determine if they contain similar information, and when results are positive, the automation is validated; finally, the web-based indicator is built as a nowcasting model that uses the automatic web-based variables as input and produces predictions about the economic variable in which we are interested.

We first applied this methodology to design and evaluate a web-based indicator about the export orientation of firms. As starting point, we proved that the predictive performance of the manual web-based variables was high (over 80% of accuracy to predict if a firm is an exporter) and at least as good as the performance achieved using traditional structural variables. Then, we automated the retrieval of the web-based variables, tested their predictive performance and validated the automatic web-based indicator of firms' export orientation, given that 96% of the prediction accuracy of the model with manually retrieved web features was replicated with the automatically retrieved web features.

Then, we worked on the design and validation of a web-based indicator of firms' engagement in e-commerce. Given the ability of our web scraping system to retrieve a large number of website features in a short period of time, a wide variety of variables that could potentially reflect if a firm offers e-commerce services or not were defined and retrieved. After balancing the sample, a model to automatically select the variables with the highest predictive power among the big quantity (161 in total) of web-variables retrieved was trained and tested. The predictive accuracy of the model was over 90%, with a 95% confidence interval that ranged from 83% to 93.4%. With these good results, the web-based indicator of firms' engagement in e-commerce was validated.

The last indicator designed in this book is about firms' survival. We hypothesized that the status of a firm's website (which we basically coded as being down, unchanged or updated) could reflect the status of the firm (active or inactive). The relation between the status of websites and the status of firms was studied by two complementary models that provided very positive results: first, the probability of a firm being active was proved to impressively increase as the level of activity in the website was higher (with probabilities of between 5 and 50-fold times higher with respect to firms whose websites were down); second, and in line with this, the hazard rates of firms whose websites were working were proved to be between 70% and 94% lower than for the case of firms whose websites were down. In the case of this indicator, the ability of web data to capture firms' survival has been verified, but the retrieval process has not been automated yet.

6.2 Implications

In this book, we have validated the use of web data to produce accurate and timely economic indicators. Concretely, web-based indicators about firms' export orientation, firms' engagement in e-commerce and firms' survival have been successfully designed. The proposed web-based economic indicators present some important advantages with respect to traditional indicators: they are fast to process and can be regularly updated; they are based on publicly accessible information available at almost any time; their cost of production is lower; their level of granularity is higher, as individual online activities can be tracked (in this case, we have tracked data from the corporate websites of each firm in our samples); and their design makes it possible to monitor and analyze the whole digital universe of firms, and this way, problems such as the generally low response rate of surveys would be solved and more reliable measures could be obtained.

These results have implications for the academia, the private sector and the public sector. From the academic point of view, a new, inexpensive and fresh source of information to predict and analyze economic phenomena has been made available. Web data can complement firms' data from other sources to understand the role played by the WWW in two important business strategies within a context of globalization: being an exporter and selling online through e-commerce. In addition, studying the characteristics and changes in corporate websites can help to understand not only business strategies and their success, but also firms' survival in the market. At the same time, this validated new source of information opens up the possibility for researchers to conduct numerous experiments and basic research for validating alternative economic indicators, which is a required step prior to their large-scale production by firms or official institutions.

In the public sector, there are implications both for the producers of economic indicators, for instance official statistics offices and other public organizations, as well as for the users, that is, policy-makers. In a context of fast changes and strong competition, the availability of timely information is crucial for policy-makers to make early informed decisions, and public producers of economic indicators should deal with this necessity. To overcome this challenge, the way of producing official statistics should be adapted. In the current era where more data than ever are daily produced and computation is incredibly advanced, this is more than possible. Indeed, our results point out the viability of making a transition towards complementing, in a first step, and transforming, in a second step, the way of doing official statistics, moving to a paradigm based on the WWW as source of data (along with other Big Data sources not used in this book) and on non-traditional methods to process such data. What is more, this transformation would imply not only processing the current official indicators in a different way, but also producing new indicators for which data were not available in the past but are available in enormous quantities in the present.

For policy-makers, to conduct a short-term monitoring of the economy would be possible. Therefore, they could earlier make informed decisions about maintaining, modifying or releasing a policy, which could contribute to a more efficient and effective use of public resources. This book sheds light on the possibility to implement a continuous monitoring about export promotion policies, public programs to promote digital sales and business de-mography, which could be done from two perspectives: on the one hand, to assess if public programs are providing the expected results; on the other hand, to detect which are the trends in trade openness, in digital business and in specific economic sectors, that is, to track whether an economic sector is ex-panding (firms are being founded) or reducing (firms are closing). All of them are crucial areas of interest for policy-makers because of their impact on the strength of an economy, given that they affect production, competitiveness and employment.

For the private sector, a new source of data from which to obtain granular, accurate information of an economic nature arises the chance to make business. Managers and administrators are increasingly demanding exhaustive and fresh information about how the sector in which their firm operate is evolving, what are competitors doing or which are the characteristics of the firm's customers. Their objectives are to anticipate changes, have a more profound knowledge of their context, and reorient the strategies of companies. Online and web data are particularly useful to this end, as they capture the daily single movements and activities of individuals and firms in the digital world. Thus, the number of firms working in data science, or which are implementing data science divisions within their self structure, is growing at a high pace.

6.3 Limitations

The research conducted in this book, although having provided encouraging results, has some limitations that are enumerated below.

First, information from the Internet has a bias. This, essentially, comes from the fact that information posted online may be false or inaccurate, as there is an important human component behind them. Firms, which are the object of study in this book, may lie in their corporate websites. For instance, they may describe activities in which they are not enrolled or services that they do not actually offer to deliberately provide a specific public image to their customers or competitors. Also, errors or lack of exactness when posting information may occur, both from the human side (for example, grammar errors) and from the machine side (for example, an error when uploading a document that makes it corrupt).

Second, online data entail a problem of representativeness, which is also considered a type of bias. Internet penetration is different in each world region, being much higher in developed than in developing countries. Additionally, the profiles of Internet users do not necessarily represent the profiles of the entire population in the world. For instance, the percentage of Internet users is not the same for each age or income range. Generally, younger people use more often the Internet than older, and people with higher income have more options to access the Internet. In the case of firms, we can only study those that have a presence on the Internet, and particularly in the case of this book, those that have a corporate website. However, with these data it is not possible to study the characteristics of firms that are not established online. Therefore, online data is not capturing the whole offline reality.

Third, the samples of firms used in this book have been selected by convenience sampling. Although it is possible to reach the entire population of companies with a website (in contrast to surveys in which sampling errors are used because accessing the whole population is not possible), we did not have the time and resources to do this throughout this book. This affects to the size of the samples and to the geographical areas represented (which comprise Spain and, for the e-commerce adoption indicator, also France). Therefore, caution should be taken when generalizing the results, as they may differ for other areas.

Fourth, to evaluate the predictive performance of the web-based export indicator, the entire sample was used instead of a train and test set. The process of training the models with part of the observations and testing their performance with different observations to obtain more robust predictions was learned during the realization of the book, and was only partially applied in the intermediate steps prior to obtaining the web-based export indicator. Afterwards, this process was completely implemented for the evaluation of the second web-based indicator that we designed (about e-commerce adoption). Furthermore, both of these indicators have been studied using cross-sectional data, so that the insights of a longitudinal analysis are not available for them.

6.4 Future work

Departing from the work developed in this book, several lines of future research have emerged.

We plan to improve our Big Data architecture to increase the level of details about the variables under study, and to automate the web-based in-dicator of firm's survival. Moreover, provided the good results obtained, we plan to extend this work and apply our methodology to study other economic activities, and also to consider other online sources besides corporate websites.

Indeed, given the importance of tourism for the Spanish economy, we are starting a research work about the viability of using online data to provide timely and more accurate forecasts of tourist arrivals.

Likewise, we are working on the proposal of a method based on applying data mining techniques to online data with the aim to monitor the results of some European public policies. To start with, we are working on the case of European Technology Platforms, which are an implementation of an R&D policy that lacks of a regular monitoring system.

Besides these lines of research, there exist many others: for instance, scraping the WWW in search of job vacancies to monitor unemployment or using search data to predict sales of products. Indeed, by the hand of Big Data, lots of possibilities of research have arisen. Thus, it is time to continue working and contributing to the fascinating field of Internet-based economic indicators.